ONNECTIONS
TO COLLEGE SUCCESS

John W. Santrock
University of Texas, Dallas

Jane S. Halonen
University of West Florida

THOMSON

WADSWORTH

Australia • Brazil • Canada • Mexico • Singapore • Spain • United Kingdom • United States

Connections to College Success
John W. Santrock/Jane S. Halonen

Executive Editor: *Carolyn Merrill*
Assistant Editor: *Eden Kram*
Development Editor: *Cathy Murphy*
Technology Project Manager: *Joe Gallagher*
Advertising Project Manager: *Brian Chaffee*
Associate Project Manager, Editorial Production: *Karen Stocz*
Print Buyer: *Betsy Donaghey*
Cover Photo: © *John Feingersh/Zefa/Corbis*

Senior Permissions Editor: *Isabel Alves*
Text Permissions Editor: *Sarah Harkrader*
Photo Manager: *Sheri Blaney*
Photo Researcher: *Christina Micek*
Senior Art Director: *Bruce Bond*
Cover Designer: *New Mediatrix*
Compositor: *Pre-Press Company, Inc.*
Printer: *Courier Kendalville*

Printed in the United States of America
1 2 3 4 5 6 7 09 08 07 06 05

Library of Congress Control Number: 2005934715

ISBN 1-4130-2265-0

Thomson Higher Education
25 Thomson Place
Boston, MA 02210-1202
USA

For more information about our products, contact us at:
Thomson Learning Academic Resource Center
1-800-423-0563

For permission to use material from this text or product, submit a request online at **http://www.thomsonrights.com**
Any additional questions about permissions can be submitted by email to **thomsonrights@thomson.com**

Brief Contents

Contents

Preface

As authors of the textbook *Your Guide to College Success* and as instructors who have worked with first-year students for many years, we know firsthand that the college success course can be a key factor in how well students master their college experience. The college success course has made a difference in the lives of thousands of students: the seemingly well-prepared student as well as the student considered at risk of dropping out, the returning student as well as the traditional-age student. Regardless of their aptitude or preparation for college, students who have taken a college success course tend to be more likely to stay in college and graduate. Along the way, they find the challenges of college—studying, building relationships, and choosing a major—less difficult because of the strategies they learned in this course.

A college course is only as good as its instructor. But an instructor benefits from good tools. In creating *Connections to College Success,* we have attempted to build a brief, accessible, and practical text, one that will serve as a helpful guide for students and a useful teaching tool for instructors. The material in *Connections to College Success* is drawn from the Fourth Edition of our text *Your Guide to College Success,* but it has been abbreviated and rethought to address the most essential elements of college success.

Connections to College Success covers the topics that are important to first-year students, including getting oriented on campus, time management, styles of learning, critical thinking, note taking, reading, studying, taking tests, communicating, building relationships, health, and planning for the future. Each chapter of *Connections to College Success* includes our much-praised "Six Strategies for Success model," as well as the following elements:

- Modular design: this approach allows students to read and digest a complete topic or concept in a succinct one- or two-page spread.
- "Links to Success": this outline opens each chapter, providing a map for students to follow while reading the chapter.
- "Making Connections": these tips for college success appear as boxed material in each chapter.
- "Applying the Strategies": these end-of-chapter projects invite students to apply what they learned in the chapter to the six strategies for success, either in their journals or on paper to turn in.
- "Putting It All Together": appearing at the end of each chapter, these exercises review chapter content and allow students to verify their comprehension of key concepts. Each chapter includes a journal exercise.
- "Evaluate Your Strategies": this feature, which appears at the end of the Introduction, is a self-assessment for students to complete and refer to as they work through the topics in the text.

Connections to College Success addresses the critical concerns faced by first-year college students in a highly readable magazine format. With this brief text, students can quickly grasp key concepts, apply proven strategies, and confirm their understanding of the material.

Instructor Supplements: See your local Thomson Wadsworth sales representative for details about available supplements.

Multimedia Manager 2007 for College Success

Whether you want to create a lecture from scratch or use a customizable template, our **Multimedia Manager for College Success** makes preparation a snap. With content that is easy to customize, this one-step presentation tool makes course preparation faster and simpler—and lectures more engaging. *Free* to qualified adopters and organized by 14 common college success topics, the Multimedia Manager helps you assemble, edit, and present tailored multimedia lectures for your course. We have updated the Multimedia Manager with new PowerPoint presentations, new video clips, new images, and new web links that can supplement your college success course.

The **Wadsworth Premier College Success Academic Planner** can be packaged with this text. This inexpensive spiral-bound day planner is also available in a customized version.

Videos: See your local Thomson Wadsworth sales representative for more information.

10 Things Every Student Needs to Know to Study (1-4130-1533-6)

This 60-minute video covers such practical skills as note taking, test taking, and listening, among others.

10 Things Every Student Needs to Succeed in College (1-4130-2907-8)

This 60-minute video compilation illustrates ten valuable and highly effective practices every student needs in order to engage in a successful college experience. Topics include successful time management, recognizing and understanding learning styles, and written/spoken communication.

Turnitin®

See your Thomson Wadsworth sales representative if you are interested in learning more about Turnitin®. This proven online plagiarism prevention software promotes fairness in the classroom by helping students learn to correctly cite sources and allowing instructors to check for originality before reading and grading papers. Turnitin quickly checks student papers against billions of pages of Internet content, millions of published works, and millions of student papers. Access to Turnitin can be provided with your textbook under special order.

Acknowledgments

We would like to thank *College Success* editor Carolyn Merrill, who provided the inspiration for this book. We are also grateful for the significant contributions of our other Wadsworth collaborators, Cathy Murphy, Eden Kram, and Karen Stocz.

We thank our spouses—Mary Jo Santrock and Brian Halonen—for their enthusiastic support of our work, patient tolerance of our work habits, and good-humored companionship.

Introduction
Develop Strategies
for Success

Success in college? It is not enough to just want to be successful. By taking an active role in mastering specific skills and strategies, you can actually shape your own success. The key to success in college is knowing what things you value and setting goals to reach them. If you know your goals, you will have no trouble deciding what you need to learn and motivating yourself to learn it. If you let your values steer you through college, you'll feel good about yourself. You'll also prepare yourself to do great things beyond college.

This book is designed around six strategies that are essential components of college success: developing meaningful values, setting and monitoring goals, getting motivated and taking responsibility, thinking and learning, building your self-esteem and confidence, and exploring careers. If you can master these six strategies and apply them in the college setting—whether in class or out of class—you will be much more likely not only to survive college but to thrive there. Maybe you already have accomplished some of these strategies. Chances are, however, that you need help with one or more of them. This book helps you assess where you are now, what you need to change, and how to change. In this chapter, we introduce the strategies.

The "Six Strategies for Success" listed to the left will help form the foundation of your success . . . not just in college, but in life. As you read each chapter, you will practice applying the strategies to each chapter topic.

Develop Meaningful Values

Just what are "values"? Values are our beliefs and attitudes about the way we think things *should* be. They involve what is important to us. We attach values to all sorts of things: politics, religion, money, sex, education, helping others, family, friends, self-discipline, career, cheating, taking risks, self-respect, and so on.

Connect Your Values with College Success

College gives you the opportunity to explore and clarify your values. Why is this so critical? Our values represent what matters most to us, so they should guide our decisions. Without seriously reflecting on what your values are, you may spend too much time in your life on things that really aren't that important to you. Clarifying your values will help you determine which goals you really want to go after and where to direct your motivation.

Sometimes we're not aware of our values until we find ourselves in situations that expose them. For example, you might be surprised to find yourself reacting strongly when you discuss religion or politics with other students. Spend some time thinking about and clarifying your values. This will help you determine what things in life are most important to you.

Forge Academic Values

College is an opportunity to discover and test your values.

Throughout your college career, you will be making many choices that reflect your values. Although your primary goal in seeking a college education may be learning about new ideas, your journey through college can also help to build your character.

Participate Fully College involves a higher level of personal responsibility than most students experienced in high school. This freedom can be alluring, even intoxicating. Especially when instructors do not require attendance, you may be tempted to skip classes. What's wrong with skipping class? First of all it's expensive—you are paying for the class you miss. Second, it harms your learning. Third, it hurts your grades. Finally, it annoys those who end up lending you their notes to copy. (If you must miss a class, be sure to borrow notes from someone who is doing well in the course!)

Participate Honorably Most campuses publish their expectations about appropriate academic conduct in the college handbook. Many colleges have adopted an honor code to promote academic integrity. This represents your formal agreement to abide by rules of conduct that promote trust and high ethical standards. Typically, codes address such problems as cheating, plagiarism (submitting someone else's work for your own), or other forms of dishonest performance. The consequences for violating the honor code may range from something as mild as "censure," to formal recognition of wrongdoing, to expulsion from school.

Why do some students make choices that put them at risk for expulsion? They engage in misdirected problem solving based on faulty conclusions:

1. *The risk of getting caught is small.* Students have witnessed lots of academic misconduct in their own careers by other students who have gotten away with it. They violate academic expectations because they assume they won't get caught either.

2. *There is no other way to be "successful."* Students may get so far behind in their work that they don't trust what they have learned to help them succeed on tests or papers. These students focus on getting an acceptable grade by any means available rather than letting the grade legitimately stand for their learning.

3. *It doesn't matter in the long run.* Some students don't see the connection between the violations of academic trust and the quality of their character development and education. Cutting corners in the classroom can eventually forge bad habits that may show up later in professional life as "cooked books," malpractice, or other violations of professional ethics.

4. *The penalty for getting caught won't be severe.* Some students take the risk because they are confident that penalties will not be imposed. They may have heard that honor code procedures discourage faculty from reporting students or they may simply believe that they will be able to fast-talk their professors out of taking a severe stance.

All of these examples illustrate how students can miss the point. Every academic performance you render gives you an opportunity to exercise your own values and demonstrate your character. Why should you embrace academic integrity and commit to doing your best?

1. *Practicing academic integrity builds moral character.* Doing the right thing often means doing the hard thing. It may mean sacrificing personal advantage to achieve an outcome for the benefit of others. However, doing the right thing also feels good in that you avoid the suspicion, guilt, and ambiguity caused by doing wrong.

2. *Choosing moral actions builds others' trust in you.* We expect others to treat us fairly and appropriately. Violating the academic trust signals to others that the character flaw you exhibit in the classroom could carry over to other settings as well.

3. *Making fraudulent grades masks important feedback about learning.* An artificially high grade may cheat you of the opportunity to recognize your learning deficits and address them appropriately before you graduate.

4. *Improving integrity in the classroom can rebuild national character.* The recent emergence of massive corporate crimes linked to greed has prompted many social critics to suggest that the country has lost its moral compass. Embracing principles of academic integrity will be fundamental to helping us resurrect our moral foundations.

Set Goals, Plan, and Monitor

Once you have determined your personal values, the next step is to set specific goals based on these values, plan how to reach them, and monitor your progress. Setting goals is directly linked to the development of values, as they influence each other throughout life.

Set Goals and Plan How to Reach Them

Let's see how you might connect your personal values with setting goals. Suppose that one of your values is being well educated. If so, then it's important for you to set educational goals and plan how to reach them. If one of your values is "contributing to the welfare of others," it is then important to set goals pertaining to this, such as participating in at least one service learning activity per month (volunteering at a nursing home for the elderly, for example).

Setting goals will pay off in helping you get done what you need to get done on time. Students who do not set goals and plan usually don't excel in college. Time tends to slip away until it's too late for them to accomplish what they want or to perform as well as they could.

Set Goals That Are Challenging, Reasonable, and Specific For every goal that you set, ask yourself, "Is it challenging? Is it reasonable? Is it specific?" When you set challenging goals, you commit to improving yourself. Be realistic, but stretch yourself to achieve something meaningful. Also, when you set goals, be concrete and precise. An abstract goal is, "I want to be successful." A precise, concrete goal is, "I want to achieve a 3.5 average this term."

Set Long-Term and Short-Term Goals Some long-term goals, such as becoming a successful teacher or getting into medical school, take years to reach. Other goals are more short-term, such as doubling study time next week or perhaps simply not drinking this weekend.

Make a Personal Plan

A goal is nothing without a means of achieving it. Good planning means getting organized mentally, which often requires writing things down. It means getting your life in order and controlling your time and your life, instead of letting your world and time control you.

Set Completion Dates for Your Goals Work out schedules to meet your goals on time. If you want to obtain a college degree, you might want to set a goal of four to six years from now as your completion date, depending on how much time each year you can devote to college. If your goal is to make one good friend, you might want to set a time of six weeks from now for achieving it.

Create Subgoals Don't let long periods of time slip by when you aren't working on something that will help you reach your goals. You don't need to do everything today, but you should do something every day. The U.S. Olympic speed-skating champion Bonnie Blair described how she thinks about and acts on goals every day: "No matter what the competition is, I try to find a goal that day and better that goal."

Say that one of your life goals is obtaining a college degree. You can break this down into either four subgoals (if you're in a four-year degree program) or two subgoals (if you're in a community college). Each subgoal can be the successful completion of a year in your degree program. These subgoals can be broken down into exams, quizzes, term papers, amount of time you plan to study each week, and so on. Be sure to assign a completion date to each intermediate step.

Anticipate and Overcome Obstacles It is a good idea not only to develop effective strategies for overcoming obstacles when they arise, but also to spend time anticipating what obstacles might come up in the future. Take stock of the next week, month, and term. Think about some problems that might appear down the road, such as inadequate math or writing skills, a shortfall of money, or a failed friendship. Developing the skills now to deal with such problems can help you cope with such obstacles to college success if they arise in the future.

Monitor Your Progress

It is important to monitor your progress toward your goals to help you discover new ways to improve your academic performance. Monitoring will improve your ability to keep up with assignments and to learn how much time it takes to do well in class.

Make daily lists of things you need to do to stay on track toward your goal, and then monitor whether you do these. After writing down your goals, place the list where you can easily see it, such as on a calendar or taped to the inside of your personal planner or address book. If after a week or month you find that you are falling behind, evaluate what you can do to get back on track.

It is also important to look at the setbacks you experience as opportunities to learn (Niven, 2001). Learn from your losses as well as your successes. Many students drop out of college because they don't know how to cope with failures and learn from them. Analyzing your successes and failures can help you better understand yourself and the changes you need to make in your life.

Get Motivated and Take Responsibility

This book describes many strategies that will help you to succeed in college, but all the strategies in the world won't help you unless you become motivated to learn them and use them. In the "Six Strategies for Success" model on page xiii, getting motivated and taking responsibility is directly linked with goal setting as the two go hand in hand in college and throughout life. In national surveys, when pitted against other factors such as intelligence and ability, how motivated people are proves to be a better predictor of career success. How can you become motivated to succeed?

Develop an Internal Locus of Control

If you take responsibility for your successes and failures, you have what's known as an internal locus of control. If you don't take such personal responsibility and let others, or luck, be responsible for what happens to you, you have an external locus of control. Being internally controlled means seeing yourself as responsible for your achievement, believing that your own effort is what gets you to your goals, and being self-motivated. Research studies have found that internally controlled students are more likely than externally controlled students to:

- Have a strong work ethic (Mendoza, 1999).
- Possess high self-esteem (Stipek, 2002).
- Be aware that their grades are strongly linked to how much effort they put forth (Wigfield & others, 2006).
- Attain a high grade point average—internally controlled students average one full letter grade higher than externally controlled students (Niven, 2001).

Being internally motivated, though, does not mean doing everything in isolation. Surround yourself with other motivated people. Ask individuals who are successful how they motivate themselves. Find a mentor, such as an experienced student, an instructor, or a teaching assistant you respect, and ask his or her advice on motivation.

Expect to Succeed and Persist until You Do

Do you expect to do poorly in college or to be highly successful? How much effort do you put into your academic work? Both expecting to succeed and persisting with a great deal of effort will positively impact how well you will do in your courses.

Being motivated not only involves having expectations for success, it also involves persistence. Getting through college is a marathon, not a 100-yard dash. Studying a little here and a little there won't work. To be successful you have to study often—almost every day for weeks and months at a time. You'll often need to make small sacrifices to gain long-term rewards. College is not all work and no play, but if you mainly play you will pay for it by the end of the term.

Build a Mission Statement

An important aspect of taking responsibility for yourself is knowing what you want to be. One way to find this out is to build a mission statement of your desires, dreams, and destiny. This involves:

- Describing what characteristics you admire in people
- Identifying your hero and why this person is your hero
- Evaluating your strengths
- Thinking about what you love to do
- Determining what matters most to you
- Discovering what you want to learn
- Pointing to your dreams for the future
- Figuring out what you want to contribute
- Knowing what inspires you

Get Involved

Successful college students are often involved in college activities (Astin, 1993). This can be accomplished in many ways—through socializing and studying with friends, engaging in extracurricular activities, living on campus, having a part-time campus job, and interacting with faculty. Students who are not involved in college activities frequently feel socially isolated and unhappy with their college experience.

Explore your values by getting to know new people, seeking out new situations, asking new questions, reading new books, and reexamining your school's catalog for new ideas and possibilities that turn on your mind. Keep track of the moments in the day when you feel the most energetic and inspired because of what you are doing or what you see and hear around you. What do these moments tell you about how to become more involved and less bored or unhappy?

Think and Learn

Above all, college is a place to think and learn, to practice thinking reflectively, critically, and productively. Evaluate, analyze, and create. Solve problems and poke holes in arguments. Be prepared to show "why" and to back up your assertions with solid evidence. Don't just stay on the surface of problems. Stretch your mind. Become deeply immersed in meaningful thinking. In the "Six Strategies for Success" model on page xiii, thinking and learning are important strategies directly linked with motivation. Get motivated to make the most of college as an opportunity to strengthen these important skills.

You learn when you adapt and change because of experience. Make it a high priority to learn from both your successes and your failures. Make a commitment to avoid making the same mistake twice. Identify your weaknesses and develop strategies for strengthening those weaknesses or working around them in a way that promotes your college success. For example, if you are not a good writer, take full advantage of the writing center on your campus.

Focus Your Talents and Master Work Skills

Some courses may put you to sleep but others will spark new interests and even make you passionate about a subject. Where you "catch fire" and become highly motivated to learn will point you to a successful future. Remember that not all learning takes place in the classroom. If a topic in class seems interesting to you, explore it more deeply.

Success in college and in life requires self-discipline and good work habits. These habits will help you become not only a better student in college but also a valuable employee, a skilled professional, or a resourceful entrepreneur afterward. These skills include knowing how to take good notes, participate in class, collaborate with other students, and interact with instructors. You also need good study and test-taking strategies and good reading, writing, and speaking skills. The following chapters will provide you with a solid foundation and extensive strategies for improving these skills.

Explore Your Learning Styles

Some people learn mainly by doing things themselves. Others learn best by watching or listening to someone lecture. Still others learn best by reading, or doing field projects or laboratory experiments. Your college experience will help you to sort through the ways you prefer to learn.

In Chapter 3, you'll explore learning styles extensively and determine those at which you excel. You'll also learn some strategies that can improve your flexibility in using different learning styles. This exploration continues throughout the book.

Manage Your Time

Learning takes a lot of time. Your life as a college student will benefit enormously if you become a great time manager. If you waste too much time, you'll find yourself poorly prepared the night before an important exam, for instance. If you manage time well, you can relax before exams and other deadlines. Time management will help you be more productive and less stressed, with a better balance between work and play. Chapter 2 is all about managing time. Among other things, it will explain how to set priorities, eliminate procrastination, and monitor your time.

Think Critically and Creatively

There is no getting around the fact that you are going to have to spend quite a bit of time memorizing material to do well in many courses. You will get the most out of your college experience, however, when you go beyond just memorizing information and think critically and creatively.

Thinking critically involves more than learning how to make sound arguments, solve problems, and make good decisions. Thinking creatively involves coming up with unique, innovative ideas and solutions to problems. We will further explore thinking critically and thinking creatively in Chapter 4.

Communicate Effectively

A very important aspect of college success and life thereafter is having effective communication skills. College will provide you with many opportunities to refine and improve your speaking, writing, and listening skills. When interviewing college graduates for prospective jobs, many employers rate communication skills as the most important factor in hiring a job candidate. We will explore many aspects of speaking and writing skills in Chapter 9, and examine listening and communication skills in relationships in Chapter 10.

Use Your Resources

An important aspect of learning is figuring out what resources are available to you and how best to use them. Your college also has many resources that can support your college success, including academic advisors, physicians, mental health counselors, and many others. Become acquainted with these resources early in your college transition and don't hesitate to use them when you think that you need help. We will extensively explore your connection to campus and ways to use college resources in the Chapter 1.

Join the Information Age

To get the most out of your college education, you need to be familiar with computers. We encourage you to take every opportunity to use computers and applications such as word processing, e-mail, and the World Wide Web effectively. If you don't already have good computer skills, developing them will make your college life much easier and improve your chances of landing a good job later. To be blunt, if you don't develop computer skills, you are likely to get left behind.

Build Self-Esteem and Confidence

Building your self-esteem and confidence will improve your performance in college and beyond, as well as make you a happier, more satisfied individual. What is self-esteem? Sometimes called self-worth or self-image, it is how you feel about you, the image you have of yourself. Many things in your life contribute to your self-esteem: how much you have succeeded or failed, how much the people around you (parents, friends, peers, teachers) positively evaluate or criticize you, whether you tend to be optimistic or pessimistic, and so forth.

Building self-esteem will give you the confidence to tackle difficult tasks and create a positive vision of the future. It will help you reach your goals and give you the confidence to act on your values. If you have low self-esteem, commit to raising it. Following are some good strategies for increasing self-esteem, based on a number of research studies (Bednar, Wells, & Peterson, 1995).

Have Confidence in Yourself Believe in your ability to succeed and do well in life. Believing that you can make changes in your life is a key aspect of improving your self-esteem. Researchers have found that confidence, in combination with a realistic self-appraisal, produces a 30 percent increase in college students' satisfaction with their lives (Sedlacek, 1999). Monitor what you do and say to yourself. Putting yourself down will only lower your self-esteem. Believe in your abilities.

Identify Causes of Low Self-Esteem Is your low self-esteem the result of bad grades? Is it because you live with people who constantly criticize you and put you down? Identifying the sources of low self-esteem and changing them is critical to increasing it.

Define Important Areas of Competence Students have the highest self-esteem when they perform competently in the areas of their lives that matter to them. If doing well in school is important to you, academic success will increase your self-esteem. If you value being well connected in society, having a great social life will increase your self-esteem.

Get Emotional Support and Social Approval When people—friends, family, classmates, and counselors—say nice things to us, are warm and friendly, and approve of what we say and do, our self-esteem improves. Seek out supportive people and find ways to give support back.

Achieve Learning new skills can increase both achievement and self-esteem. For example, learning better study skills can improve your grade point average (GPA). This, in turn, might do wonders for how you feel about yourself this term and may also pay off in the long run.

Cope Self-esteem also increases when we tackle a problem instead of fleeing. Coping makes us feel good about ourselves. When we avoid coping with problems, they mount up and lower our self-esteem.

Explore Careers

Exploring careers now will help you link your short-term and college goals with some of your long-term life goals, and help you be motivated by your long-term prospects. What do you plan to make your life's work? Is there a specific career or several careers that you want to pursue? If you have a career in mind, how certain are you that it is the best one for you?

An important aspect of college is training for a career. Each of us wants to find a rewarding career and enjoy the work we do. If you're a typical first-year student, you may not have any idea yet of which particular career you would like to pursue. That's okay for right now, especially if you're currently taking a lot of general education courses. But as you move further along in college it becomes ever more important to develop such ideas about your future. The sixth and final point in the "Six Strategies for Success" model on page xiii is exploring careers. This strategy links back to the first point, developing meaningful values, demonstrating the interconnectedness of all six strategies for success.

Choosing a career based on a college education will likely bring you a higher income and a longer, happier life. College graduates can enter careers that will earn them considerably more money in their lifetimes than those who do not go to college (*Occupational Outlook Handbook*, 2006–2007). In the United States, individuals with a bachelor's degree make over $1,000 a month more on average than those with only a high school diploma. Individuals with two years of college and an associate degree make over $500 a month more than those who only graduated from high school. Over a lifetime, a college graduate will make on average approximately $600,000 more than a high school graduate will! College graduates also report being happier with their work and having more continuous work records than those who don't attend or don't finish college.

How would you like to give yourself several more years of life? One of the least known ways to do this is to graduate from college. If you do, you will likely live longer than your less-educated counterparts. How much longer? At least one year longer. And if you go to college for five years or more, you are expected to live three years longer than you would if you had only finished high school.

A successful career often involves three things:

1. Gaining specialized knowledge of the content of a particular field (like electrical engineering or English).
2. Having good work skills, especially those involved in communication and computers.
3. Having good personal skills, including being able to get along with people, maintaining high self-esteem, and working from one's own values, motivations, and goals.

Your college experiences will give you plenty of opportunities to develop your talents in these three areas. Throughout this book other connections to the long-term question of careers will be made, and Chapter 12 is devoted to this topic.

Evaluate Your Strategies

The "Six Strategies for Success" model visually demonstrates the interconnectedness of these important strategies that you can use to form the foundation of your success. The first step is to evaluate where you stand now with regard to implementing these strategies for success in college.

Place a checkmark next to each of the following statements that represents you and your actions now. Award yourself one point for each checkmark. Then add up the points for each of the six sections. You can use these totals as a guide for working through the strategies in each of the chapters that follow.

Develop Meaningful Values

1. ____ I know what my values are.
2. ____ I feel good about my values.
3. ____ I have reflected on what values I want to guide my life.
4. ____ I have discussed my values with others.
5. ____ My values are helping me succeed in college.
6. ____ My values serve as a foundation for the goals I want to achieve.
7. ____ I've been in situations in which my values have been tested and I stayed with them.
8. ____ I have a clear understanding of my purpose in life.
9. ____ I am flexible and realize that my values might change.
10. ____ My values are at the core of my existence.
    ____ TOTAL

Set Goals, Plan, and Monitor

1. ____ I am good at setting goals.
2. ____ I have established some long-term goals.
3. ____ I have created subgoals to go along with my long-term goals.
4. ____ The goals I have set are challenging but reachable.
5. ____ My goals are concrete and specific.
6. ____ I periodically monitor my progress toward reaching the goals I have set.
7. ____ I have set completion dates for these goals.
8. ____ I manage time effectively in the pursuit of my goals.
9. ____ I make lists of things I need to do to stay on track in reaching my goals.
10. ____ I anticipate and overcome obstacles on the way to reaching my goals.
    ____ TOTAL

Get Motivated and Take Responsibility

1. ____ I am internally motivated.
2. ____ I take responsibility for my actions.
3. ____ I expect to succeed.
4. ____ I am persistent at completing important tasks.
5. ____ I am passionate about succeeding in life.
6. ____ I put a lot of energy into college.
7. ____ I have a strong work ethic.
8. ____ If I get bored, it doesn't last long.
9. ____ I have a strong desire to be a competent person.
10. ____ I am good at staying on task and not being distracted.
    ____ TOTAL

Think and Learn

1. ____ I am self-disciplined and have good work habits.
2. ____ I have good study skills.
3. ____ I know the best ways I can learn.
4. ____ I am good at managing my time.
5. ____ I think critically.
6. ____ I think creatively.
7. ____ I have good problem-solving skills.
8. ____ I communicate effectively with good speaking and listening skills.
9. ____ I know what learning resources are available and how best to use them.
10. ____ I have good computer skills.
    ____ TOTAL

Build Self-Esteem and Confidence

1. ____ I have a lot of confidence in myself.
2. ____ I feel good about myself.
3. ____ I have a positive self-image.
4. ____ I have a lot to be proud of.
5. ____ I am a person of worth.
6. ____ When I don't feel good about myself, I can tell why and attempt to do something about it.
7. ____ If I start to feel bad about myself, it doesn't last long.
8. ____ I have a good support system and get good feedback from others.
9. ____ My achievements help me feel good about myself.
10. ____ I have good coping skills.
    ____ TOTAL

1. ____ I know how much more successful I am likely to be if I complete college.
2. ____ I have several careers that I would like to pursue.
3. ____ I know what my college major will be.
4. ____ My college major matches up well with the careers I am interested in.
5. ____ I have good communication skills.
6. ____ I have good personal skills, including being able to get along with others.
7. ____ I know which college experiences will help me down the road in my pursuit of a career.
8. ____ I have talked with a career counselor about careers that might interest me.
9. ____ I have set some career goals.
10. ____ I am on the right path to reaching those career goals.
____ TOTAL

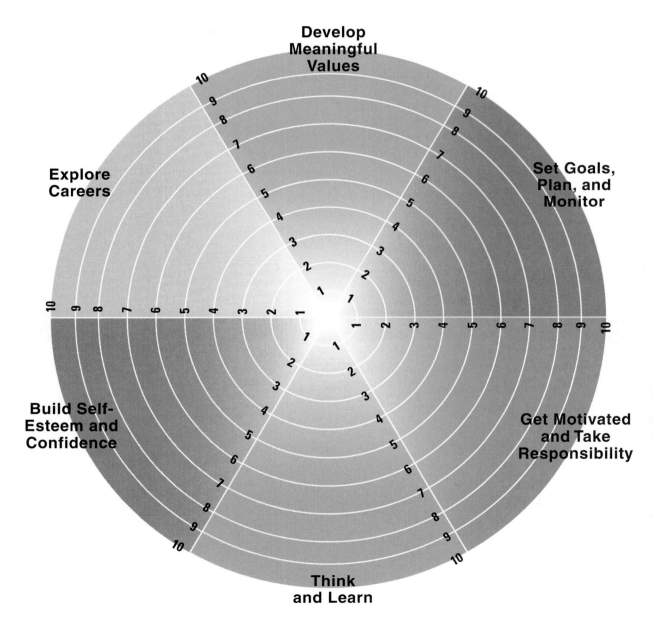

1 ⟩ Explore College

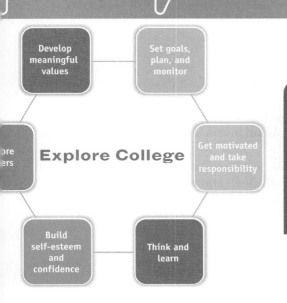

Develop meaningful values

Set goals, plan, and monitor

Explore College

Get motivated and take responsibility

Build self-esteem and confidence

Think and learn

ore rs

As you read, think about the "Six Strategies for Success" listed to the left and how this chapter can help you maximize success in these important areas. For example, to master college and reach your goals, you need good resources. Important resources include knowledgeable and helpful people on campus, such as academic advisors, more advanced students, and mentors. If you connect effectively to these resources, your college life will be easier, less stressful, and more productive.

Make the College Transition

Life is change and college is change. Whether you have entered college right out of high school or as a returning student, you'll need to adapt to this new place. What unexpected things are going on around you? What's different? What changes are you going through as you make this transition?

The Transition into College

When you think of your first year of college, what comes to mind? Does beginning your college experience give you a greater sense of freedom, or do you feel more scheduled? Do you have more control of your time, or less? A feeling of certainty about your future, or uncertainty? Where you came from—directly out of high school, the world of work, or raising a family—will influence your answer.

If you were in high school last year, you will notice the following differences between high school and college:

- *College classes are much larger, more complex, and more impersonal.* Your teachers in high school probably knew your name and maybe even your family. In college, however, your instructors may not know your name or recognize your face outside class.

- *In college, attendance may be up to you.* Although some of your instructors will require attendance, many won't. If you miss class, it's your responsibility to find out what you missed. Most instructors do not allow makeup work without a reasonable, well-documented explanation.

- *College instructors give fewer tests.* They may hold you responsible for more than what they say in class. Some won't let you make up tests.

- *In college, nobody treats you like a kid anymore.* You have more independence, choices, and responsibility. You are more on your own about how you use your time than you were in high school.

- *You have to do much more reading in college.* More of your work will need to be done outside class. You may be expected to make your own decisions about what information from your reading is most important for you to remember.

- *Good grades are harder to get in college.* In many colleges, there is more competition for grades than in high school, and instructors set the bar higher for an A or B.

- *Your college classmates may be more diverse in age and backgrounds.* Look around. You'll probably see more older individuals and more people from different cultures than you did in your high school.

An increasing number of students start or finish college at an older age (Sax & others, 2004). More than one out of five full-time and two-thirds of part-time students today are returning students. Some work full time, are married, have children or grandchildren, are divorced, retired, or changing careers. Some have attended college before while others have not.

If you have entered or returned to college at an older age, you may experience college differently from recent high school graduates.

- *You have more commitments.* You may have to balance your class work with commitments to a partner, children, a job, and community responsibilities. This means you may have less flexibility about when you can attend classes. You may need child care or have special transportation needs.

- *You may feel underqualified.* As an older student, you may lack confidence in your skill and abilities or undervalue your knowledge and experience.

- *Your contributions are unique and valuable.* These include a wide range of life experiences that you can apply to issues and problems in class.

- *You develop different priorities.* Your multiple commitments may stimulate you to be more skilled than younger students in managing your time. You may have greater maturity in work habits and more experience participating in discussions. You may also face setbacks more easily. Failing a pop quiz, for instance, is not likely to feel devastating for those who have experienced greater disappointments in life.

making connections | Returning Student Strategies

Evaluate your support system
A strong and varied support system can help you adapt to college. If you have a partner or family, their encouragement and understanding can help a lot. Your friends also can lend support.

Make new friends
As you seek out friends, focus on meeting other older students. You'll find they also juggle responsibilities and are anxious about their classes.

Get involved in campus life
The campus is not just for younger students. Check out the organizations and groups at your college. Join one or more that interest you.

Don't be afraid to ask for help
Learn about the services your college offers. Health and counseling services can help you with the special concerns of older students. These include parenting and child care, divorce, and time management. If you have any doubts about your academic skills, get some help from the study skill professionals on your campus.

Map Out an Academic Path

Whatever your background prior to college, it is important for you to devote some time to designing an academic path. Your academic advisor is an important resource for helping you with this process. Contact your advisor whenever you have any questions about your academic life.

Connect with Your Academic Advisor

Talk with your academic advisor about course requirements that can help you realize your plans. Advisors can explain why certain courses are required and can alert you to instructors suited to your preferred learning style. Plan to confer with your advisor regularly. When it's time to register for the next term's courses, schedule a meeting with your advisor early in the registration period.

Bring a tentative plan of the courses that you think will satisfy your requirements. Be open if the advisor offers you compelling reasons for taking other courses. For ex-

Your academic advisor is one of your most important resources.

ample, your advisor may suggest that by taking some harder courses than you had planned, you can prepare yourself better for the career you have chosen. Your advisor will help you reach your career objective as efficiently as possible, but not by compromising solid preparation.

Some advisors may not have regular office hours. To maximize your effectiveness and efficiency, call or e-mail your academic advisor for an appointment before dropping by. If you put your concerns in writing before the appointment, your advisor will have some time to work on your specific issues before you arrive.

If the "chemistry" between you and your academic advisor isn't good, confront that problem by discussing what behaviors make you feel uncomfortable. Recognize that your own actions may have something to do with the problem. You need an advisor you can trust. If you can't work out a compromise, request a change to find an advisor who is right for you.

Get to Know Your College Catalog

A college catalog is a valuable resource. You can get a printed copy from your academic advisor or find it on your campus web site. College catalogs usually are published every one or two years. Be sure to save the catalog that is in effect when you enroll for the first time. Why? Because requirements for specific programs sometimes change, and you usually will be held to the degree plan that was in place when you enrolled. Be sure to look at the following sections of your catalog:

- *Major.* A major, or field of concentration, is a series of courses that provides a foundation for deep understanding of an academic discipline. Ideally, your major will match up with your career interests, goals, and values. Your advisor can help you investigate majors that interest you. Most students do not know for sure what they want to major in until they finish the first year of college.

  Majors vary in the number of courses they require. Know what yours requires so that you can plan each term and graduate on time.

- *Requirements.* The catalog should tell you what the core requirements are for any major you are interested in, whether there are any prerequisites for the programs, and whether there is a sequence of courses you should follow.

- *Prerequisites.* Many courses have prerequisites and other enrollment requirements, such as "consent of instructor," "enrollment limited to majors," "seniors only," "honor students," and so on. You are expected to comply with these prerequisites and enrollment requirements when you register for courses.

- *Core courses.* These are the central courses that all students must take, either for general education requirements or for a major.

- *Electives.* In addition to core courses, you will be able to take electives, courses that are not required. You can take electives in your major and outside of it. Through electives you can explore your interests and expand your education beyond the fundamentals.

Get the Right Courses

With a little effort, you can learn how to select courses that satisfy your requirements and your interests. Here are some strategies for making sound selections:

- *List your constraints.* You might have child-care responsibilities, an inflexible work schedule, or commuting issues. If so, block out the times you can't take classes.

- *Examine your interests.* Interests are activities that you like to do. In many ways, they are what you truly are passionate about (Combs, 2002). Notice how you react to different activities. When you are interested in something, you are alert, tuned in, engaged, and curious. Time often passes quickly when you are doing something you are passionate about. When you aren't interested, you become bored, your mind wanders, and you tune out.

- *Study your options.* Colleges have lists of classes required for various specialty diplomas or majors. Examine the college catalog to determine which courses are required for both general education requirements and for the specialty or major that you want to pursue.

- *Register for a reasonable course load.* Many colleges do not charge for additional courses beyond those needed for full-time status. You might be tempted to pile on extra courses to save time and money. But think again. By taking too many courses, you may spread yourself too thin.

- *Take the right mix of courses.* Don't load up with too many really tough courses in the same term. Check into how much reading and other time is required for specific courses. If you can't find anyone who can tell you this, make appointments with the instructors. Ask them what the course requirements are, how much reading they expect, and so on.

- *Ask the pros.* The "pros" in this case are students who are already in your preferred program. Ask their advice about which courses and instructors to take.

Connect with Your Campus

It costs you nothing to connect with your campus, yet nothing will help you more than knowing and using your campus resources. You probably have visited some of them already—the bookstore for textbooks and study supplies, the student center or commons to check out bulletin boards or pick up a newspaper. An important goal in college is learning how to solve your personal problems and get your needs met. Many campus resources can help you attain these goals. You can learn a great deal about the best campus resources if you make this an important goal and aren't afraid to ask questions.

Get Help When You Need It

Coming prepared to meetings with your instructor will make a positive impression.

Most people on campus will be eager to help you in your quest to master college. Whether you want information or training, here are some things you can do to get the help you need (Canfield & Hansen, 1995):

- *Ask as though you expect to get help.* Your tuition dollars pay for assistance in the classroom, the library, or even the cafeteria line. Ask with authority. You may be able to enter that restricted part of the library merely by acting like you know what you're doing. High self-esteem gives you the confidence to do these kinds of things.

- *Ask someone who is in a position to help you.* You may have to do some homework to find out who can help you best. If someone you approach can't deliver, ask whether that person knows of someone else who might be able to help you. Form a network of resources.

- *Ask clear and specific questions.* Even those who enjoy helping students don't like to have their time wasted. Think ahead about what you need and what level of detail will satisfy you. Take notes so you won't have to ask twice.

- *Ask with passion, civility, humor, and creativity.* Enthusiasm goes a long way toward engaging others to want to help you. A polite request is easier to accommodate than a loud, demanding one. Be humorous and creative where appropriate, but size up whether your instructors will appreciate a joke before you make one.

Find Personal Support Services

Seek counseling for personal concerns. College life is often challenging on a personal level. Talking to a counselor or therapist may provide the relief you need. Large campuses have mental health departments or psychology clinics. They may have therapists and counselors on site who will give you the support you need on a one-to-one or a group basis. The fee for such services may be on a sliding scale (meaning that the cost is proportional to your income), covered by your health insurance policy, or covered by your tuition.

Some student services offer topic-specific support groups, such as a group for single mothers returning to college or one for students struggling with English as a second language. In support groups you can meet others who have problems similar to yours. Ask the counseling center or dean's office about support groups on campus.

Pursue Extracurricular Activities

Participating in extracurricular activities improves your chances of meeting people who share your interests. Activities may be listed in the campus handbook or advertised in the student newspaper. You can join the club for your academic major. If you're interested in journalism, you can work on the college newspaper or yearbook. Prospective drama students can audition for plays. Students interested in business can join an entrepreneur's group to examine how business people manage their lives and work. Intramural and campus sports also are available. Some clubs promote service to others. Fraternities and sororities are also available.

It may seem as if your study life is too full to accommodate fun. However, leisure activities are important for balance in your life. Extracurricular activities of any kind can also help you develop leadership skills and learn to manage multiple commitments.

Enrich Your Cultural Life

Your campus and community may offer unique opportunities for cultural enrichment. Because most campuses are training grounds for artists and performers, they often operate an art gallery for student work or invited artists, host live performances in music, dance, and theater to showcase student and faculty talent, and bring in professional performers from the community. Museums, galleries, theaters, the symphony, and political gatherings off campus can all enrich your college experience.

Many college students also have spiritual concerns. Campus ministries usually coordinate religious activities for various denominations. These may be formal religious services or social groups where you can simply get together with others of a similar faith. You not only can practice your faith but also expand your network of friends with common values.

Obtain the Tools You Need

In addition to connecting with the people and groups that will make your college experience richer, be sure you have the tools you need to succeed academically. These tools include knowing how to navigate the campus library, being comfortable using a computer, and getting learning support when you need it.

Tap the Library

The sooner you get a feel for how the library works, the more useful it will be to you. One of your classes may arrange a tour. If not, ask a librarian for help in getting oriented.

Although librarians may look busy when you approach them, step up and ask for help. Most of them enjoy teaching others how to use the library. If you find an especially friendly librarian, cultivate the relationship. A librarian friend can be a lifesaver.

What do you need to know in order to use the library effectively? The following questions may help you organize your first tour:

How can I check out materials?

What are the penalties for late returns?

Do instructors place materials on reserve? How does this work?

What interesting or helpful journals does the library have? Are they available online?

Is the library catalog online or on cards? What can I access electronically?

Can I arrange interlibrary loans to get materials from other libraries?

What kinds of reference materials are available? Are the abstracts of published research on microfilm or in books?

Where are "the stacks" and when can I use them?

What technological resources does the library have that will help me succeed in college?

Connect with Computers

If you've had little chance to become familiar with computers, now is the time to do so. Become computer literate by making good use of the free computer labs on campus, many of which are open early and close late to promote student access. Take some beginning computer classes that will help you get started using e-mail, surfing the World Wide Web, and using a word processor, spreadsheet software, presentation software, graphics programs, and databases. Or find part-time work that involves computers so you can earn a paycheck while you learn these valuable skills.

In 2004, 78 percent of first-year students reported that they used the Internet for research or homework and this percentage is likely to increase (Sax & others, 2004). If you have not personally experienced the astounding capabilities of the Web, find ways to gain access and get good at using it. One way to do this is to contact the learning resources center at your college and ask about courses or tutorials on Internet use.

E-mail allows ongoing Internet conversations with people who share your interests. In 2003, 64 percent of first-year students said that they communicate via e-mail. In college you'll find that some of your instructors may require discussions online using a class listserve. Such discussions allow you to practice the language of the course and can improve your understanding of course concepts. Some instructors welcome questions via e-mail because it's often more convenient than office hours for both parties. Your campus may provide you with a free e-mail account. If not, you can join a full-range commercial service for $20 per month or less.

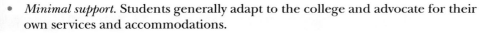

Overcome Limitations

Most campuses provide access to specialists who can assist you with academic problems.

Study skills specialists can diagnose learning difficulties, suggest compensating strategies for your assignments, and give you direction about taking courses with instructors who are more sympathetic with your struggle to learn. They also can set up and monitor additional study supports, including tutoring and study groups, to get you accustomed to the demands of college-level work.

More than 10 percent of college students have some form of physical or mental impairment that substantially limits their major life activities. Colleges are required to make reasonable accommodations to allow students with a disability to perform up to their capacity. Accommodations can be made for motor and mobility impairments, visual and hearing deficits, physical and mental health problems, and learning disabilities.

If you have a disability, determine what support you need to succeed in college. Colleges provide many levels of support:

- *Minimal support.* Students generally adapt to the college and advocate for their own services and accommodations.
- *Moderate support.* The campus offers a service office or special staff to help students with advocacy and accommodations.
- *Intense support.* The campus provides specific programs and instructional services for students with disabilities.

Among the academic services that may be available on your campus are:

- *Referrals for testing, diagnosis, and rehabilitation.* Specialists who can help in this area may be located on or off campus.
- *Registration assistance.* This involves consideration regarding the location of classrooms, scheduling, and, in some cases, waivers of course requirements.
- *Accommodations for taking tests.* Instructors may allow expanded or unlimited time to complete tests and you may be able to use a word processor or other support resources during the exam.
- *Classroom assistance.* Someone may be assigned to take notes for you or translate lectures into sign language. Instructors may allow their lectures to be taped for students with impaired vision or other disabilities.
- *Special computing services and library skills.* Support services on campus are finding inventive new ways to interpret written texts to overcome reading and visual limitations.

Putting It All Together

1. Consider your roommate or another student you have met recently. How do the challenges you both face making the transition to college differ? How are they similar?

2. What are some key aspects of designing an academic path? List three things you can do *now* to begin this process.

3. Where would you go to find help with the following issues?

   a. You have to write a report on global warming.
   b. You are having trouble managing your courses, work schedule, and family commitments.
   c. You don't know what major to choose.
   d. You would like to make some friends among the other students.
   e. You don't have the computer skills you need for your courses.

4. In your journal or on paper to turn in, reflect on the people who have helped you most on campus so far. Who are they? How have they helped you? In what areas do you still need help? Where can you get that help?

2 Manage Your Time

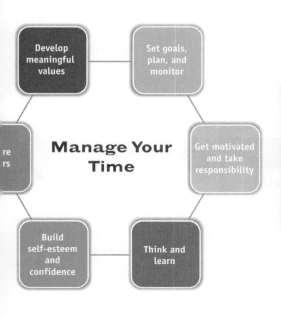

Develop meaningful values

Set goals, plan, and monitor

Get motivated and take responsibility

Think and learn

Build self-esteem and confidence

Manage Your Time

As you read, think about the "Six Strategies for Success" listed to the left and how managing your time can help you maximize success in these important areas. For example, to reach your goals and still be able to live a balanced life, you need to do two things: **(1)** Discipline yourself to plan and monitor your time with your values and goals in mind. **(2)** Take steps to minimize procrastination and distractions.

Spend It Wisely

It's your time. Make the most of it.

You can reap many benefits by managing your time effectively:

- *Be more productive.* Using your time more effectively will increase your productivity in college, and you will get better grades.

- *Reduce your stress.* The day before an exam you suddenly realize that you have a massive amount of studying to do. Panic! Tension builds and stress escalates. Effectively managing your time will help you reduce the stress in your life.

- *Improve your self-esteem.* Learning to manage time effectively will make you feel successful and ahead of the curve. Wasting a lot of time will make you feel discouraged about yourself because you are constantly playing catch up.

- *Achieve balance in your life.* Developing good time-management skills and actively using them will give you more time for school, work, home, family, and leisure.

- *Establish an important career skill.* In most careers, to be successful you'll not only need to complete many different tasks, but also need to complete them quickly and by a deadline.

- *Reach your goals.* You need time to reach your goals, so the better you can manage time, the bigger you can dream.

Avoid Time Wasters

Vilfredo Pareto's *80–20 principle* states that about 80 percent of what people do yields about 20 percent of the results, whereas about 20 percent of what people do produces about 80 percent of the results. For example, approximately 80 percent of people's mail (e-mail and postal mail) is junk and best not read at all. Only 20 percent is important. Although 20 percent of the newspaper may be worth reading, the other 80 percent should just be skimmed. Separating the important stuff from the junk will help you become a better time manager.

How often do you surf the Web, daydream, socialize, worry, or procrastinate? Is it hard for you to say "no" to a request for your time? This can lead to wasting a lot of time in low-priority rather than high-priority activities. It's your time. Spend it wisely.

Decide what you need to do and what you can realistically do. Say "no" to everything else. If this is difficult for you, write "NO" in large letters on a card and place it next to the phone, computer, or on your desk (Yager, 1999). You might suggest someone else who could do what is asked or offer to do it when you have more time.

Avoid telephone and e-mail time wasters:

- Use an answering machine or voice mail to screen incoming calls.
- Learn to say, "I can't talk right now. Can I call you back?" Set aside a time to return calls.
- When you leave a message, give a specific time for someone to return your call so that you avoid playing telephone tag.
- Set a specific time to check your e-mail every day or two rather than responding to each message as it is received.
- Change your computer settings so messages don't pop up in the middle of important projects such as writing a paper or doing homework online.

Know Your Rhythms

Evaluate yourself. What time of day are you most alert and focused? For example, do you have trouble getting up in the morning for early classes? Do you love getting up early but feel drowsy in the afternoon or evening?

If you're a night person, take afternoon classes. Conduct your study sessions at night. If you're a morning person, choose morning classes. Get most of your studying done by early evening. What can you do if you hate getting up early but are stuck with early morning classes? Start your day off properly. Many students begin their day with too little sleep and a junk-food breakfast, or no breakfast at all. Does this description fit you?

Try getting a good night's sleep and eating a healthful breakfast before you tackle your morning classes. You may even discover that you're not a night person after all. Exercise is also a great way to get some energy and be more alert when you need to be—and is often more effective than caffeine.

Choose a Strategy

Two strategies for getting the most out of your week are called *Swiss cheese* and *set time*. Time management expert Alan Lakein (1973) describes the Swiss cheese approach as poking holes in a bigger task by working on it in small bursts of time or at odd times. For example, if you have 10–15 minutes several times a day, you can work on a math problem or jot down some thoughts for an English paper. You'll be surprised at how much you can accomplish in a few minutes.

If you're not a cheese lover, the set time approach may suit you better. In this approach, you set aside a fixed amount of time to work on a task. In mapping out your weekly plans, you may decide that you need to spend six hours a week reading your biology text and doing biology homework. You could then set aside 4–6 P.M. Monday, Wednesday, and Saturday for this work.

Plan for the Term

You'll benefit enormously by mapping out a week-by-week plan for the entire term. The two basic types of planning tools available are paper-and-pencil planners and electronic planners. Paper-and-pencil planners let you see at a glance a day, a week, or an entire term. Electronic planners such as a Palm personal digital assistant (PDA) or a smart cell phone are compact and can sort, organize, and store information more efficiently than a paper-and-pencil planner. They can even provide audible reminders of when to do things.

If you are gadget-oriented, learn technology easily, and can afford it, you might want to consider an electronic planner or smart cell phone. If you are not, the paper-and-pencil planner is more than sufficient.

If you don't already have a calendar for the term, use the grid on page 15 to create one. Somewhere on the page, list the five values that are the most important priorities of your life. Also list the five most important goals you want to attain this term. Then write in the weeks and number the days. Note vacations and holidays, employment, family commitments, commuting time, and volunteer work on your calendar. Next, get out your course syllabi and write down dates and deadlines for exams, major homework assignments, and papers.

After you've scheduled your exams and other tasks on the calendar, look at the dates. Think about how many days or weeks you'll need to study for major exams and write major papers. Mark the days or weeks in which these tasks will be your main priorities. Refer often to the values and goals you listed at the top of the page when allocating your time for this term. Your term calendar is not etched in stone. Check it regularly and modify it as necessary. An instructor might add another assignment or change a test date. You might find out that you need more study time than you originally predicted for a particular course, or that your work schedule or family responsibilities change during the term.

Term Planner

Week of	MONDAY	TUESDAY	WEDNESDAY	THURSDAY	FRIDAY	SATURDAY	SUNDAY
_____							
_____							
_____							
_____							
_____							
_____							
_____							
_____							
_____							
_____							
_____							
_____							
_____							
_____							
_____							
_____							

Make a Weekly and Daily Plan

Make a Weekly Plan

In addition to creating a term plan, a weekly plan also will help you maximize your time. Use the grid below or your own planner.

Ask yourself these questions about the next week: What do I expect to accomplish? What will I have to do to reach these goals? What tasks are more important than others? How much time will each activity take? When will I do each activity? How flexible do I have to be to allow for unexpected things?

In the *Plan* column on the grid, fill in your class hours, study hours, regular work commitments, family commitments, and other routine tasks. Then fill in the remain-

Weekly Planner

		MONDAY		TUESDAY		WEDNESDAY	
		Plan	Actual	Plan	Actual	Plan	Actual
AM	6:00						
	7:00						
	8:00						
	9:00						
	10:00						
	11:00						
PM	12:00						
	1:00						
	2:00						
	3:00						
	4:00						
	5:00						
	6:00						
	7:00						
	8:00						
	9:00						
	10:00						
	11:00						
AM	12:00						
	1:00						
	2:00						
	3:00						
	4:00						
	5:00						

der of the things you plan to do next week. Fill in the *Plan* column at the end of the preceding week. The plan takes no more than a half hour for most students to complete, yet it can save you at least an hour a day that week! During the week, monitor your schedule closely to see whether you carried out your plans. A good strategy is to sit down at the end of each day and write in the *Actual* column what you actually did that day and compare it with what you planned to do. Analyze the comparison for problems and plan some changes to solve them.

Use the weekly planner in concert with your term planner each week of the term. Every weekend, pull out your term planner and identify your most important priorities for the following week. Make any changes that are needed and then do the same thing with your weekly planner to help stay focused.

Create a To-Do List

Great time managers figure out what the most important things are for each day and allocate enough time to get them done. Figuring out the most important things to do involves setting priorities. An effective way to do this is to create a manageable to-do list. Your goal is to complete at least all of your priority items on the list. A no-miss day is one after which you can cross off every item. If that turns out to be impossible, make sure that you finish the most important tasks first.

THURSDAY		FRIDAY		SATURDAY		SUNDAY	
Plan	Actual	Plan	Actual	Plan	Actual	Plan	Actual

Conquer Procrastination

Procrastination often hurts many students' efforts to become good time managers. Do you recognize yourself in any of the following forms of procrastination (University of Illinois Counseling Center, 1984)?

- *Ignoring the task, hoping it will go away.* A midterm test in math is not going to evaporate, no matter how much you ignore it.

- *Underestimating the work involved in the task or overestimating your abilities and resources.* Do you tell yourself that you're such a great writer that you can grind out a 20-page paper overnight?

- *Spending endless hours on computer games and surfing the Internet.* You might have fun while you're doing this, but will you have to pay a price?

- *Deceiving yourself that a mediocre or bad performance is acceptable.* You may tell yourself that a 2.8 GPA will get you into graduate school or guarantee a great job after graduation. This mindset may deter you from working hard enough to get the GPA you really need to succeed after college.

- *Substituting a worthy but lower-priority nonacademic activity.* You might clean your room instead of studying for a test. Cleanliness may be "next to godliness," but if it becomes important only when you need to study for a test, you are procrastinating.

- *Believing that repeated "minor" delays won't hurt you.* You might put off writing a paper so you can watch *Six Feet Under* or a wrestling match.

- *Dramatizing a commitment to a task rather than doing it.* You take your books along on a weekend trip but never open them.

- *Persevering on only one part of the task.* You write and rewrite the first paragraph of a paper, but you never get to the body of it.

- *Becoming paralyzed when having to choose between two alternatives.* You agonize over whether to do your math or English homework first, and neither gets done.

Here are some good strategies for overcoming procrastination:

- *Put a deadline on your calendar.* This creates a sense of urgency.

- *Get organized.* Some procrastinators don't organize things effectively. Your term planner, weekly planner, and to-do list will come in handy here.

- *Divide the task into smaller jobs.* Sometimes we procrastinate because the task seems so complex and overwhelming. Divide a larger task into smaller parts. Set subgoals of finishing one part at a time. This strategy often can make what seemed to be a completely unmanageable task an achievable one.

- *Take a stand.* Commit yourself to doing the task. One of the best ways to do this is to write yourself a "contract" and sign it. Or, tell a friend or partner about your plans.

Achieve a Balance

Time management is particularly challenging for college students who also hold a job, have a partner or children, or commute.

Balance College and Work

If possible, obtain financial aid so that you do not have to work while in college. Students who work full time are less likely than those working part time or not at all to complete college, have high grade point averages, graduate with honors, or go on to graduate school (Astin, 1993). If you need to work, try to work no more than 10 to 20 hours. Full-time students who work more than 20 hours a week get lower grades than students who work fewer hours. They are also much more likely to drop out of college.

Try to work on campus. Students who work part time on campus will likely be connected with other students and faculty, which more than compensates for the time they devote to the part-time job. Carefully consider how many classes you are taking and how much work each one requires. You might want to take a reduced class load to give you more time for studying and work.

Students who work on campus are more likely to excel than those who work off campus.

Balance College and Family

Time is especially precious if you have a spouse, partner, or children. Communicating and planning are important assets in balancing your family time and academic time. Set time aside for your partner. Plan ahead for tasks that require extra study time. Inform your partner about test dates and other deadlines and post a copy of your term plan on the refrigerator or in another prominent place.

Try to do some studying while you're at school. Use time between classes, for example. Plan to arrive at school 30 minutes before your first class and stay 30 minutes after your last class to squeeze in uninterrupted study time. If your child has homework, do yours at the same time. Take a break for 10 minutes or so for each hour you study at home, and play or talk with your child. Then go back to your studying. If your children are old enough to understand, tell them what your study routine is and ask for their cooperation.

Consider having your children play with neighboring children during your study hours. If your children are young, this might be arranged under another parent's supervision. Or try to swap child care with other student parents. Also check into child-care and community agencies that may provide service and activities for your children in the before-school and after-school hours.

- Save time by consistently using to-do lists and weekly plans.
- Audiotape your instructors' lectures, if allowed. Play them back on the way home or on the way to school.
- Each day on your way to work, school, or home, rehearse what you learned in class.
- If you carpool with classmates, use the commuting time to discuss class material with them.
- Use a backpack or briefcase to carry books and papers that you use each day. Organize these materials the night before to make sure you have everything you need.
- Early in the semester, exchange phone numbers and e-mail addresses with other students in your classes. Call them if you need to discuss class issues or their notes for a class you missed.
- Create a personal commuter telephone and/or e-mail directory. Important phone numbers and addresses might include your instructors and their secretaries or teaching assistants, the library, student services, study partners, and various campus resources.

Applying the Six Strategies for Success

How does the material in this chapter make you think about ways you can succeed in college, particularly in the area of time management? Write down your personal insights from reading the chapter that help you make meaningful links to the six strategies for success described on page 11.

Putting It All Together

1. **Who's in Charge?**
   We discussed many different ideas about managing time, such as developing a term plan, creating a weekly plan, setting priorities, consistently creating to-do lists, and tackling procrastination.

   - What are your current strengths and weaknesses with regard to managing time?
   - What do you plan to do to address your weaknesses?

2. **The 80–20 Principle in Your Academic Life**
   Recall our description of the 80–20 principle earlier in this chapter, which stated that approximately 80 percent of what people do produces about 20 percent of the results they achieve, and vice versa. Think about the courses you are taking this term. How might you apply the 80–20 principle to work more efficiently?

3. **Change a Habit**
   Select a bad habit that is hurting your ability to effectively manage time. Many people find that in managing time, it helps to replace a bad habit with a new, more positive habit. What positive habit can you substitute for your bad habit?

4. **Link Goals with Time Spent in Activities**
   In your journal or on paper to turn in, write responses to the following:

   - In what waking activities do you spend more than three hours a week?
   - How does each of these activities relate to your goals?
   - Examine your reasons for participating in activities that are unrelated to your goals.

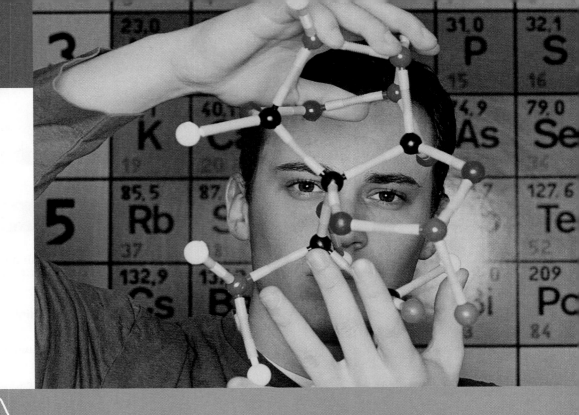

3 — Diversify Your Learning Style

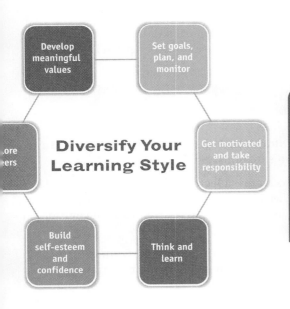

Develop meaningful values

Set goals, plan, and monitor

ore ers

Diversify Your Learning Style

Get motivated and take responsibility

Build self-esteem and confidence

Think and learn

All of us learn a little differently, according to individual abilities, preferences, and characteristics. To reach your goals, it's important to understand how you learn and to look for ways to become more versatile. As you read, think about the "Six Strategies for Success" listed to the left and how this chapter can help you maximize success in these important areas, particularly "Think and Learn."

Know Your Preferences

Multiple Intelligences

The psychologist Howard Gardner (1989) proposed that intelligence consists of several types of abilities. Gardner now suggests that these sorts of abilities cluster in at least eight different areas, or *domains:*

1. *Verbal-Linguistic Skills:* sensitivity to and appreciation of word meanings and the function of language

2. *Logical-Mathematical Skills:* orderly use of reasoning, logic, and mathematics to understand and explain abstract ideas

3. *Musical Abilities:* appreciating, performing, or creating music or the elements of music, such as rhythm or pitch

4. *Bodily-Kinesthetic Awareness:* coordinated and skilled use of objects in the environment, involving both gross and fine motor skills

5. *Spatial Skills:* accurate perception and reproduction of spatial images, including strong navigation and artistic skills

6. *Intrapersonal Abilities:* meaningful discrimination and interpretation of the behavior and moods of others

7. *Interpersonal Abilities:* accurate self-perception, including a refined capacity to identify and represent complex personal emotions and motives

8. *Naturalist Abilities:* understanding, relating to, classifying, and explaining aspects of the natural world

Gardner argues that these domains are independent, so humans can be highly developed in one area but not others. You may be naturally more gifted in some areas than in others.

Sensory Preferences

Your sensory preference for receiving information also contributes to your learning style and how easily you learn in different situations.

Auditory Learning *Auditory learners* absorb a lecture without much effort. They may not even need to take careful notes, as they learn just by listening. Auditory learners may avoid making eye contact with anyone in the class so they can concentrate on catching every word and nuance.

Visual Learning *Visual learners* have an easier time learning from lectures with visual components such as pictures, diagrams, cartoons, or demonstrations. They make images of words and concepts and then capture these images on paper for a quick review. Visual learners benefit from the use of charts, maps, notes, and flash cards when they study.

Tactile or Kinesthetic Learning

Some people are *tactile* or *kinesthetic learners.*

They prefer touch as their primary mode for taking in information. Unfortunately, very few college classes provide an opportunity for tactile learners to use their preferred sensory mode. Art, recreation, and technical classes related to careers involving manual procedures are among the most prominent exceptions. In auditory learning situations, tactile learners benefit by writing out important facts and even tracing their notes with their fingers.

Kinesthetic learners excel at hands-on activities.

Learning Preferences

People also differ in how they like to learn and think about ideas. Here are four distinctive ways based on David Kolb's (1984) work on experiential learning.

Learn by Doing Although some people can learn passively simply by listening, watching, or reading, those with active learning preferences fare better when they learn by doing, through problems or games and simulations, for example. They like to apply principles through fieldwork, lab activities, projects, or discussions. Classes that are ideal for learning by doing include science and math classes as well as career-oriented classes, such as business and nursing.

Learn by Reflecting Reflecting here means having an opportunity to compare incoming information to personal experience. Reflective learners prefer classes such as the humanities that tend to be rich in emotional content. Reflective learners often show preferences for learning by listening, because these situations provide the least interference for thoughtful, quiet reflection.

Because they look carefully at a situation and think about its meaning, reflective learners often set reasonable goals and achieve them. Because they're good at problem solving and decision making, they like to set their own goals for learning (Jonassen & Grabowski, 1993). Reflective students tend to enjoy journal writing, project logs, film critiques, and essay questions, and prefer intimate discussions of content to group discussions.

Learn by Critical Thinking Critical thinkers like learning situations that encourage them to grapple with ideas in ways that push beyond memorizing facts. They enjoy manipulating symbols, figuring out unknowns, and making predictions. They like to analyze relationships, create and defend arguments, and make judgments. Critical thinkers often are good with abstract ideas, and enjoy classes that are theoretical in nature or emphasize logical reasoning, model building, and well-organized ideas. Good critical thinkers perform especially well in courses that appeal to verbal-linguistic, logical-mathematical, and naturalist intelligences.

Learn by Creative Thinking In contrast, creative thinkers thrive in learning situations that offer opportunities for unique personal expression. Although humanities and arts classes particularly develop creative thinking, creative opportunities can be found in other courses, too, because creative thinking can be expressed in all domains of multiple intelligence. Creative thinkers prefer to write stories, brainstorm, solve problems in original ways, design research, and so forth. They think more holistically, meaning that they try to consider a broad range of information in their problem solving.

Know Your Personality

Your personality is made up of your enduring personal characteristics. Your personality style can facilitate or hinder your success in the classroom. We'll examine two popular approaches to understanding how personality affects learning: the Five Factor Personality Model and the Myers-Briggs Type Indicator.

Five Factor Personality Model

Many psychologists today believe that five basic dimensions of personality are consistently demonstrated by people across cultures (Costa & McCrae, 1995). Each dimension represents a continuum and is described below, along with an overview of how these dimensions can impact success in college. To remember all five dimensions, remember the word *OCEAN:*

O: Open to experience High-O people are adventurous, imaginative, and unconventional. They tend to enjoy classes where they can experiment with new ideas. Low-O people are conventional, conservative, and rigid in their thinking, preferring more highly structured learning situations.

C: Conscientiousness High-C people are hardworking, ambitious, and driven. They tend to have developed work habits likely to place them on the dean's list. Low-C people are pleasure seeking, negligent, and irresponsible, making them more vulnerable to being placed on probation or being suspended.

E: Extraversion High-E individuals (extraverts) are high-spirited and energetic, thriving on the continuous opportunity that college provides to meet and work with different people. Low-E individuals (introverts) are reserved and passive, tending to seek less social stimulation to do their best work.

A: Agreeableness High-A people are good-natured, trusting, and helpful. They tend to be well liked and respected and may have an easier time negotiating positive outcomes to conflicts. Low-A people are irritable, suspicious, and vengeful. They are less likely to get any breaks when negotiating because they tend to approach conflict with a hostile attitude and low expectations of others.

N: Neuroticism High-N individuals suffer a variety of problems related to emotional instability, such as anger, depression, and impulsiveness, which can create constant chaotic conditions that can threaten academic survival. Low-N individuals adapt well, tolerate frustration, and maintain a more realistic perspective. They tend to have developed personal resources that can help them garner success and rebound from failure.

Myers-Briggs Type Indicator (MBTI)

Another popular approach to understanding the role of personality in academic success is the Myers-Briggs Type Indicator (MBTI) (Myers, 1962). The MBTI identifies four dimensions of personality functioning by measuring responses to a series of questions that ask for a preference between two alternatives:

1. *Extraversion/Introversion (E/I)* measures students' social orientation. Extraverts (E) like talking with others and taking action. Introverts (I) prefer to have

others do the talking. (This is similar to the "open to experience" dimension addressed in the Five Factor Model.)

2. *Sensing/Intuiting (S/N)* explores how students process information. Sensers (S) are most at home with facts and examples; they are drawn to realistic, practical applications. Intuiters (N) prefer concepts and theories, which can give greater play to imagination and inspiration.

3. *Thinking/Feeling (T/F)* emphasizes how students make decisions. Thinkers (T) like to take an objective approach and emphasize logic and analysis in their decisions. Feelers (F) prefer emotion to logic; they give greater weight to the impact of relationships in their decisions.

4. *Judging/Perceiving (J/P)* taps how students achieve their goals. Judgers (J) prefer clearly defined strategies to achieve their goals and may jump to closure too quickly. Perceivers (P) like to consider all sides to a problem and may be at some risk for not completing their work. (This also taps similar characteristics to the "openness to experience" dimension in the Five Factor Model.)

Your personality profile can be configured from your preferences on the four dimensions of the MBTI. The test captures your style using a four-letter code that communicates your preferences on each dimension. For example, the "ENTJ" code reveals an extravert with a preference for an orderly pursuit of concrete details but a reliance on intuitive decision making. In contrast, the "ISFP" represents the style of someone who is drawn to solitary activities, relying on facts and emotions.

As you can imagine, students with these contrasting styles are unlikely to be equally happy in any one class. For example, consider how students with different personality styles might relate to a highly structured classroom. Structure would be much more appealing to the introvert who relies more on orderly process than the extravert who prefers spontaneity; the extravert would have to do much more work to adapt to the highly structured classroom.

Find out about your MBTI profile from the campus counseling or career center. The inventory should be administered and interpreted by trained MBTI examiners, although an online version of this inventory, the Keirsey Temperament scale, can be found on the Internet at <http://www.keirsey.com/frame.html>. Avoid relying on the results of personality tests, however, in a way that restricts your options or limits your horizons. Instead, use personality test results to help you identify blind spots in your thinking and increase your adaptability.

FIGURE 3.1 MBTI Styles in the Classroom

This Style . . .	Prefers classes that emphasize . . .	But can adapt best to unfavorable conditions by . . .
Extraverts	active learning, group projects	forming a study group to meet their social needs
Introverts	lectures, structured tasks	setting manageable social goals (for example, contribute to discussions once every two weeks)
Sensers	memorizable facts, concrete questions	identifying key abstract ideas and theories along with their practical implications
Intuiters	interpretation, imagination	identifying the most important facts and figures
Thinkers	objective feedback, pressure to succeed	seeking extra feedback from the instructor to create feeling of external pressure
Feelers	positive feedback, individual recognition	seeking extra time from the instructor to create personal connection
Judgers	orderliness, structure, and deadlines	setting own deadlines and structure
Perceivers	spontaneity, flexibility	assuming a temporary role of a student who must be rigidly organized to be successful

Work with Your Instructors

Much of college is about interactions with your professors, and the success of these interactions will have a major impact on your overall success in college.

Now that you know more about how to assess your personality and learning preferences, you will be much better equipped to deal with your instructors. Also, this knowledge should provide you with a bit more feeling of control. If you know what your strengths and weaknesses are, you are better able to improve on the weaknesses and build on the strengths.

Adapt to Your Instructor's Teaching Style

The next time you register for class, invest some time in identifying which instructors have a teaching style that suits your learning style. Interview seasoned students. Ask how the instructor teaches. For example, does the instructor lecture the entire period or involve the class in discussion? Does she use active learning strategies? Does he offer outlines or other supports? Teaching styles are every bit as diverse as learning styles. Teachers will vary not only in their disciplines but also in their enthusiasm, competence, warmth, eccentricities, and humor. In addition, we can divide instructors into two types:

The Student-Centered Teacher Some instructors focus more on developing students' intellectual growth. They run their classes with a variety of activities chosen to motivate student interest and heighten learning. They might use small group discussions, film clips, technology, and student performance as part of their teaching. The student-centered teacher tends to appeal to individuals who are open to experience, like hands-on activities, and have energetic, extraverted approaches to learning.

However, you might prefer the structure and efficiency of a well-designed lecture, particularly if you're a good auditory learner, you like to memorize "the facts," or you tend to be introverted. If so, what can you do to survive the student-centered class?

- Outline your reading.
- Try to anticipate what the course will cover.
- Talk with the instructor about the course and how it's working for you.
- Form a study group to work more systematically on the key ideas.

The Content-Centered Teacher Content-centered teachers typically use lectures as their primary teaching method. The learning climate in lecture-based courses is highly structured, paced by the lecturer's strategy for covering material in a meaningful way. The content-centered approach tends to appeal to auditory learners who prefer classes that minimize involvement with peers. In fact, students who thrive in these environments might well consider college teaching as a potential career.

Visual and tactile learners or learners who prefer active or more social learning experiences simply have to work harder to adapt their

Meeting with your instructors during office hours will help you resolve differences between your learning style and their teaching style.

learning style to the demands of content-centered courses. If you face this challenge, what can you do to succeed in a content-centered class?

- Learn to make systematic, creative notes or at least work with the notes creatively when you study.
- Generate practical examples that help you form concrete connections with the course material.
- Form a study group that can help you talk about and play with course concepts.

Make a Good Impression

College instructors expect you to have academic common sense. Knowing how to develop relationships with your instructors is an important part of that common sense. Here are some tips for getting off on the right foot.

Bring the right books and supplies to class.

Prepare for class by reading the assignments beforehand.

Get to know your instructor by asking questions during class and making visits during office hours.

Do your work on time.

Use the syllabus to follow the progress of the course and to prepare for exams.

Ask courteous questions, be respectful, and behave with maturity.

Maintain your academic integrity by not cheating or plagiarizing.

making connections

Become a Distinctive Student

Sit in the front
The most motivated and interested students often sit close to the instructor to minimize distractions and create the opportunity for informal discussion before or after class.

Bring to class articles or clippings related to the course
Instructors like to see you make independent connections between what you're learning and your life outside the classroom. They may incorporate your ideas into the class and remember you for making the contribution.

Take advantage of existing opportunities to get to know your instructors informally
On some campuses, faculty members sponsor informal gatherings to help you network with others. You also can join student clubs with faculty sponsors. These are great opportunities to get to know the faculty as people.

Visit during your instructor's office hours
Most instructors identify their office hours when the course begins. Check in with your instructor about something you found interesting or were confused about from class discussion. Ask the instructor to review your notes to see whether your note-taking skills are on target.

Use e-mail to connect, if that is an option
Many instructors like to communicate with their students via e-mail. This is a great option if you're shy or the instructor seems hard to approach.

Actively seek a mentor
After you engage an instructor's interest in you, find out about the instructor's availability to serve as your mentor—someone who can give you guidance beyond the classroom and help you find other opportunities to develop. This can be the most meaningful personal connection you make in college.

Make a Major Decision

A college degree can be a passport to a professional career, but a well-chosen major can also produce a great number of opportunities that are linked to your interests and skills. Your learning style should influence which career you pursue and the major you choose to help you get there.

Link your natural intellectual talents to possible majors and career options. Gardner's theory of multiple intelligences has been used to explore the relationship between intellectual ability and career choice.

Every college major tends to emphasize certain intellectual strengths, learning preferences, and personality styles more than others. Consider these examples:

- Marcia has a particular talent for music. She prefers the kind of hands-on learning in her music classes over courses where she passively takes notes on concepts. Her auditory skills are especially well developed. Because she is also effective at working with others, her major of music education represents a natural outgrowth of her skills *(musical and interpersonal intelligences; auditory sensory preference; learn by doing; extraversion/high-agreeableness personality style).*

- Darnell enjoys classes where he can sit, listen, and think carefully about the issues. He especially enjoys writing assignments that allow him to reflect on the significance of ideas, particularly if he has to take apart an issue and form some judgments. He enjoys learning new and complex words. He is thinking about opting for a journalism major *(verbal-linguistic and intrapersonal intelligences; auditory sensory preference; learn by reflecting and critical thinking; thinking/perceiving personality style).*

- Carra enjoys taking risks. She likes to combine her strengths in mathematics and her growing ability to deal effectively with others in action-oriented projects. She learns best when she can apply principles in hands-on situations. Carra believes a business major will complement her entrepreneurial style *(logical-mathematical and interpersonal intelligences; tactile sensory preference; learn by doing; open to experience personality style).*

- Bruce has never been a big fan of reading or writing, but he keenly appreciates courses that allow him to be physically active. He likes the hands-on activities that his kinesiology classes offer and is considering a career in recreation management *(bodily-kinesthetic awareness intelligence; tactile sensory preference; learn by doing; extraversion/sensing personality style).*

- Portia has a vivid visual imagination. She prefers classes where she can express her creative impulses. She is thinking about a career in graphic design but knows she has some work to do to develop her interaction skills for business success *(spatial intelligence; visual sensory preference; learn by creative thinking; intuitive/low-agreeableness personality style).*

FIGURE 3.2 **Intelligent Career Choices**

The theory of multiple intelligences suggests that intellectual strengths predict career choices. Review some traditional and less-conventional careers linked to different domains of intelligence.

Intelligence Domain	Traditional Careers	Less-Conventional Careers	Intelligence Domain	Traditional Careers	Less-Conventional Careers

Verbal-Linguistic	author
	reporter
	teacher
	librarian
	attorney
	advertising
	  specialist
	politician
		talk-show host
		poet
		children's
		  book writer
		crossword
		  puzzle maker
		campaign manager
			Musical	performer
				singer
				music teacher
					composer
					conductor
					sound effects
					  specialist

Logical-Mathematical	engineer scientist mathematician statistician insurance specialist computer expert claims adjuster	physicist astronomer astronaut	Spatial	engineer architect surgeon painter sailor Web designer fashion designer	mapmaker sculptor billboard designer
Intrapersonal	novelist psychologist philosopher	advice columnist feature writer	Bodily-Kinesthetic	artisan actor athlete dancer coach	professional juggler professional skater health writer

Interpersonal	politician
	social worker
	sales manager
	psychologist
	public relations
	  specialist
	nurse, doctor, or
	  other health
	  care giver
		religious leader	Naturalist	conservationist
				agricultural
				  specialist
				floral designer
				museum curator
				librarian
				botanist
					safari director
					antique specialist
					baseball card expert
					game-show winner

Putting It All Together

1. List the eight types of intelligence that Gardner identified and circle the one that best represents you. How can you use this information to enhance your success in college?

2. List the three types of sensory preferences for learning and circle the one that best represents you. How can you also use this to enhance your college success?

3. List the four types of experiential learning preferences and circle the one that best represents you. Now consider the preferences you circled for #1 and #2. What does this imply about the types of courses in which you might be most successful?

4. In your journal or on paper, list your strengths and weaknesses across the inventories. What new insights do you have about your learning potential? What is one positive change you can make based on your knowledge that will enhance your success?

4 ⟩ Expand Your Thinking Skills

Develop meaningful values

Set goals, plan, and monitor

Expand Your Thinking Skills

Get motivated and take responsibility

ore ers

Build self-esteem and confidence

Think and learn

Learning to think well provides a solid foundation for succeeding in college assignments and in any current or future career. As you read, think about the "Six Strategies for Success" listed to the left and how this chapter can help you maximize success in these important areas, particularly "Think and Learn."

Think Critically

When a teacher offers you a chance to practice the higher-order skill of thinking critically and evaluating, it's easy to feel intimidated. However, some strategies can help you handle it.

Engaging in discussion helps you improve your critical thinking skills.

1. *Decide whether you like what you're being asked to judge.* Your general reaction can set the stage for detailed analysis later on.

2. *Look for both positive and negative attributes.* Some people unnecessarily limit their thinking by focusing only on the attributes that support their emotional response. Make sure you look for support for the other side.

3. *Use criteria to stimulate your thinking.* To what degree is the work you are evaluating effective? Sufficient? Adequate? Logical? Design your own criteria for evaluating an argument.

4. *Use examples to support your judgment.* Expect to explain your judgment. Be specific in pointing out areas that support your position.

Reason, Infer, and Evaluate Claims

Sometimes you may find that you don't have all the information you need to understand a phenomenon, make a prediction, or solve a problem. Through reasoning, you can derive the missing elements. Good reasoners effectively make inferences, use logic, and create and defend arguments (Beyer, 1998). Good reasoning isn't always easy, but it can be learned.

Instructors may challenge you to sort fact from fiction. They may ask you to judge the *validity* (truthfulness) of a *claim* (a statement that can be either true or false but not both) (Epstein, 2000). Claims are different from *facts*, which are truths that can't be disputed.

Fact: The moon is full at least once a month.

Claim: The full moon makes people a little crazy.

Notice how the claim is debatable and requires evidence before we can determine its validity; the fact cannot be challenged. When you evaluate a claim, you have three choices:

1. Accept the claim.
2. Reject the claim.
3. Suspend judgment until you have more information.

When to Accept a Claim There are three circumstances in which it's reasonable to accept a claim: you can trust your *personal experience* as evidence of its truthfulness; the claim comes from a *trustworthy expert;* or it comes from a *reliable media source.*

When to Question a Claim Question claims that: come from "unnamed sources"; confer an advantage to the person making the claim; are used to sell a product; offer personal experience as "proof"; are based on the claim that "everybody is doing it"; use language to mislead or "spin" the truth.

Refine Your Reasoning

You can improve your reasoning skills in the following ways:

Be Willing to Argue You may have to present a position in a term paper, in a speech, or in answer to a complex question in class. Don't shrink from those opportunities, even if you have negative feelings about the word *argument* based on the tension that you've felt when in conflict with a friend or loved one. Intellectual arguments can generate passion, too, but they need not have the same emotional intensity or feelings of personal risk as differences you have with loved ones.

Use Inductive and Deductive Reasoning There are two types of argument: induction and deduction. *Induction* involves generalizing from specific instances to broad principles. For example, perhaps you really enjoyed your first college foreign language class. Based on that experience, you might reason inductively that *all* language classes in college are great. Notice that your conclusion or rule—your induction—might be incorrect, because your next course may turn out to be disappointing.

Inductive arguments are never 100 percent certain. They can be weak or strong. In contrast, *deduction* moves from general situations or rules to specific predictions or applications. Deductive reasoning parallels the hypothesis testing procedures used in the sciences. For example, your chemistry professor may ask you to identify an unknown substance. By applying specific strategies of analysis, you narrow the possibilities until you know what the substance is. A deductive argument is 100 percent true if the premises are true and the reasoning is sound. When the premises are untrue or the logical connection between the premises and the conclusion is shaky, a deductive argument may be false.

Check Your Assumptions It's easy to reach wrong conclusions from wrong assumptions. Have you ever gotten into an argument over something you heard someone say, only to find out later that the person was joking or being ironic? In that case, your assumption—that the speaker was being truthful—was incorrect. Identify your assumptions and then do your best to verify them.

Know Your Own Bias We all have strong preferences and prejudices that may prevent us from evaluating an argument fairly. By acknowledging your own preferences and prejudices, you can increase the likelihood of coming up with more effective arguments. For example, if you know that you feel strong sympathies for single parents, you can take this bias into account when you evaluate government policies that affect their lives. Good reasoners guard against their own "soft spots" to increase their objectivity.

Take Time before Concluding Sometimes we short-circuit our reasoning. It's easy to get excited about a bright idea and stop the hard analytic work involved in thinking the problem through to the end. A premature judgment may work out, but it tends to make us even less exacting the next time we analyze a problem. Careful reasoners resist impulsive judgments. They thoroughly review an argument to make sure they have addressed all questions.

Solve Problems

Being in college will offer an array of problem-solving circumstances. Where do I get the cheapest textbooks? What field should be my major? How will I make friends who will support my academic goals and future dreams? How will I ever complete three term papers at the same time? Where can I park without getting a ticket? And then there's the "Grand Problem" you will eventually have to solve: What will I do *after* college? Your experience in solving problems in college will be critical to your future success in professional life.

making connections   Ask Questions

You can improve your analytic skills by learning to ask questions that will help you break open the ideas you're studying (Browne & Keeley, 1990). Here are some questions that can help you strengthen these important skills.

What are the issues and the conclusion?
What are the reasons?
What words or phrases are ambiguous?
Are there value conflicts?
What assumptions are being made?
What is the evidence?
Are there other ways to explain the results?
Are there flaws in the reasoning?
Is any information missing?
Do the conclusions fit the reasons?
How do the results fit with my own values?

Source: From M. N. Browne & S. M. Keeley, *Asking the Right Questions: A Guide to Critical Thinking*, 3rd Edition. Copyright © 1990 by Prentice-Hall, Inc.

Find the IDEAL Solution

Good problem solving requires a great deal of thought, and a step-by-step approach often makes that process easier. Many people find it helpful to use a specific problem solving system, such as the five-step IDEAL method (Bransford & Stein, 1984):

1. *Identify the problem.*
2. *Define the problem.*
3. *Explore alternative approaches.*
4. *Act on the best strategy.*
5. *Look back to evaluate the effects.*

How might this approach work to solve a common problem in a college setting? Let's look at a typical case.

1. *Identify the problem.* Bernita discovered when she arrived at her first art appreciation class that her instructor had already started. The instructor looked distinctively displeased as Bernita took a seat in the back of the class. When she looked at her watch, Bernita discovered that she was two minutes late. Obviously, she didn't want to annoy her instructor by arriving late to class each day. How could she avoid being late?

2. *Define the problem.* Be as specific and comprehensive as you can in defining a problem. Outline the contributing factors. There are two parts to this problem. First is the fact that the professor is clearly a stickler about being on time to his class. The second is Bernita's lateness. Why does the professor start right on time? Does he always? What made Bernita late to class? Was her watch broken? Was she carrying 60 pounds of books? Did she walk too slowly? Probably the main factor was the distance between the art appreciation class and the English class that Bernita had on the other side of the campus in the previous period. Even if she walked at top speed, she couldn't get to the art class on time.

3. *Explore alternative approaches.* Systematically gather and explore alternative solutions to isolate the best approach. Assuming that arriving late to class makes her uncomfortable enough to take action, what are some reasonable alternatives that Bernita could pursue? She can drop either class, or transfer into another section that prevents the conflict. She can talk to the instructor in her art class. Maybe there was something unusual about this day and he is usually more relaxed. He may be more understanding about her late arrival if he sees that she has a legitimate reason. Or she can ask the instructor to wait until she gets there (maybe not). Or perhaps she can talk to the English professor about leaving a couple of minutes early.

4. *Act on the best strategy.* Take specific action to resolve the problem. Include more than one strategy. Bernita decided to explain to her art instructor why she would be a few minutes late to class, added that she would do her best to get there on time, and asked for her instructor's support. The instructor verified that Bernita would be late only by two minutes and asked that she sit near the door to minimize disruptions. He also thanked Bernita for her courtesy.

5. *Look back to evaluate the effects.* The final step is to evaluate whether or not your solution works. You might be thrilled with how well it works and feel free to move on to your next challenge. Or you might discover that the solution didn't work. In this instance, Bernita's problem solving was successful. Her solution not only saved her from the trouble and expense of dropping the class but also gave her a better personal connection with her instructor.

Cultivate Problem-Solver Characteristics

What are some other ways you can maximize your problem-solving skills (Whimbey & Lochhead, 1991)?

- *Observe carefully.* Try to identify all the relevant factors in a problem from the outset. Superficial observation misses factors that hold keys to ultimate solutions. Careful observation involves analysis—identifying the relationships among the elements of the problem.

- *Stay positive and persistent.* Don't be beaten by frustration. Search for ways to make the struggle invigorating rather than frustrating.

- *Show concern for accuracy.* Pay attention to detail. It's easy to let small errors occur in moments of inattention. Take care not to leave out crucial information. Proofread statements and recheck calculations before submitting your work for review.

To solve problems, be observant, persistent, and precise.

Make Good Decisions

Solving problems often requires making good decisions. Some decisions have far-reaching consequences. For example, you decided where to go to college. To make that decision, you may have used some systematic criteria. Perhaps you wanted a college close to home with low tuition costs and specific majors. Or you may have decided to go to the campus you liked best when you visited, or the one that was just the right distance from home. How satisfied you are now with your college experience may reflect how carefully you made that decision.

Good decision makers know why they need to make a decision and examine as many options as appropriate. They consider both short- and long-term consequences of their decisions. Good decision makers articulate the pros and cons of each option and weigh the advantages and disadvantages according to their values. They choose an option that makes the most sense given the significance of the decision. Making decisions involves not only using higher-order thinking skills but also integrating those skills with values and self-knowledge. Good decisions solve problems and make life better. Bad ones often make a mess.

Four common problems interfere with good decision making: snap decisions, narrow thinking, sprawling thinking, and fuzzy thinking (Swartz, 2001).

Avoid Snap Decisions

We are inclined to make decisions too quickly, before we have had time to consider all of the options. Hasty decisions are much more likely when we are trying to solve short-term problems, leaving us vulnerable for long-term problems. You might take the first job offer you get. Although the offer might be a good match for your skills, such a quick decision precludes another alternative that might be even better.

Expand Narrow Thinking

We may simplify choices in a way that overlooks a broader array of options. Our rush to choose from column A or B may keep us from turning the page to see many other options in columns C–F. Many students feel pressured to establish their careers. You might decide advertising, for example, is the way to proceed and not consider any other options that might be more satisfying.

Contain Sprawling Thinking

We may entertain too many options. By attending to too many possibilities, we may neglect the in-depth consideration that might make the best option stand out. If you find yourself making job interview appointments with more recruiters than you reasonably can prepare for, you may be suffering from sprawling thinking.

We may not think through a problem carefully to isolate the key factors that will lead to a solution. If you find yourself struggling at midterm with diffuse feelings of failure, fuzzy thinking may be a problem. Try to systematically identify the factors that might be contributing to your problem. Perhaps you are taking too many credits to be successful? Maybe there is an instructor whose methods set your teeth on edge? You might be struggling from sleep deprivation linked to your roommates' snoring. Perhaps a broken heart might be affecting your concentration. The more specifically you can differentiate relevant factors, the more easily you can come up with a game plan that might address the issue.

Sprawling or fuzzy thinking can lead to frustration.

making connections

We're Only Human

All of us make bad decisions from time to time. How can you avoid everyday errors that produce bad decisions (Halpern, 1997)?

Avoid overconfidence
Be a little skeptical when you evaluate how wise your past decisions have been. You may be convinced that you chose exactly the right place to start your college education. You can't be completely positive, however, because you won't have any way to compare how you might have felt starting on other campuses.

Look for evidence to disconfirm
We tend to look for evidence to support the outcome that we prefer. We also tend to ignore information that might change our minds. For example, you may be eager to take a particular course because you have heard great things about the instructor. However, you may not have thought to ask questions that might weaken the case: Just how long *is* the required term paper? Good decision makers actively look for evidence that could prove them wrong so that their final decisions cover all the bases.

Distinguish wishes from reality
In the throes of optimism, we can mistakenly assume that we can will what we want to happen. For example, you may think that because you worked so hard your instructor couldn't possibly hand out the grade that your test scores predict. Think again. Good decision makers recognize that merely wishing for positive outcomes won't make it so.

Abandon sunken costs
Once you've embarked on a course of action, especially if you've had to invest time or money, it may be hard to recognize a bad decision and choose a different course. For example, if you've worked your hardest and just can't seem to do well in a particular class, don't stay there just because of the time you have already invested unless you have a good strategy that could make things change positively. Forget the time and energy you've already sunk—they're gone!

Don't overreact to forceful positions
Most people hate to be told what to do. Even if we might actually like a course of action, our preferences get squashed when someone tells us we *must* take that course of action. Good decision makers don't choose a lesser-quality alternative just to demonstrate their freedom of choice. They evaluate the quality of the suggestion apart from the manner of the person making the suggestion.

Overcome hindsight bias
Suppose you're in a class where the instructor seems a bit erratic. Toward the end of the term, he fails to show up for class and another instructor reports that he quit for mental health reasons. You might think, "I knew it all along." This pattern is referred to as *hindsight bias*. Good decision makers don't waste time claiming they predicted what has become obvious.

Source: Diane Halpern, *Critical Thinking across the Curriculum*. Copyright © 1997 by Lawrence Erlbaum Associates, Inc. Reprinted by permission of the publisher.

Think Creatively

Creative people tend to have some common characteristics (Perkins, 1984):

- They actively pursue experiences that are aesthetically pleasing. For example, they enjoy experiencing beauty in art or elegance in a scientific theory.
- They enjoy taking a unique approach to research, choosing new and exciting topics rather than going over more familiar territory that other students might address.
- They love the process of creating. For example, creative students may feel as good when they turn their work in as when they get back a successful grade.
- They are flexible and like to play with problems. Although creativity is hard work, the work goes more smoothly when taken lightly; humor greases the wheels (Goleman, Kaufmann, & Ray, 1992). Playing helps them stay open to more possibilities and disarms the inner censor that often condemns ideas as off-base.

Despite the stereotype that creative people are eccentric, most strive to evaluate their work fairly. Whether they use an established set of criteria or generate their own, they themselves ultimately judge the value of what they have created. Creative students thrive when they think of guidelines for assignments as a launching point for their imagination.

Break the Locks

Many people believe that they can't lead creative lives. You may be one of them. Despite childhoods filled with imaginative play, many of us surrender our sense of curiosity over time, harming our capacity for creativity. A variety of "mental locks" can prevent us from pursuing creative responses. Some of these locks and the "keys" for opening your mind include:

A creative approach to your coursework can make learning more inspiring.

I have to have the right answer. Sometimes the "right" answer isn't as much fun or as satisfying as an alternative.

I must be logical. But I need to get in touch with my emotional side.

I must follow the rules. But breaking the rules can be really liberating!

I have to be practical. But not in every situation.

Play is frivolous and wastes time. And I miss it! I want those feelings back!

That's not my area. But it could be!

I must avoid ambiguity. But ambiguity can open new doors.

I can't appear to be foolish. But foolishness can be fun.

To err is wrong. I'm designed to derail from time to time.

I'm not creative. But I could be!

Source: Derived from Roger Van Oech, *A Whack on the Side of the Head: How You Can Be More Creative,* 1998.

A flexible attitude sets the stage for creativity in school and throughout your life.

Foster Creativity

Psychologists affirm that anyone can be creative if they adopt the right attitudes and behaviors (Sternberg & Lubart, 1995). The following basic steps can contribute to more creative and fulfilling lives:

1. *Don't accept other peoples' blueprints.* Question assumptions. Constantly look through and around problems to find a new approach. By moving away from how most people approach things, you may find yourself in the lead. For example, if everyone executes a PowerPoint presentation for a speaking assignment in a class, you will stand out by using the blackboard or newsprint to support your key ideas. Think about how others will execute an assignment and, within reason, choose a course that makes your work stand out positively.

2. *Be vigilant about what others can't see.* Look for new and intriguing ways to redefine the environment. Use your unique past experiences to help you pick up on things that other people will miss.

3. *Differentiate the good from the bad.* Creative people will generate many possibilities but not all of them will be appropriate. Don't linger on the ideas that have weak potential.

4. *Take the plunge before you are an expert.* You don't really need to know absolutely everything about something before coming up with some new connections. In fact, sometimes too much knowledge can produce stereotyped ways of looking at the relevant facts and lead to more mundane solutions.

5. *Concentrate on the big picture.* Attending to details will help you get your creative idea across the finish line, but adopting a more holistic, global approach will help you pursue a creative lifestyle.

6. *Take sensible risks.* All creative people face obstacles. Successful creative people overcome them. Having courage and staying open to new experiences will contribute to selecting reasonable risks. Creative people take risks and learn from their mistakes. Picasso created more than 20,000 paintings; not all of them are masterpieces. Your learning will be limited if you don't stick out your neck once in a while. If you're considering a particularly creative approach to an assignment, however, share your plan ahead of time.

7. *Motivate yourself intrinsically.* If you concentrate on the joy of the process rather than the prospect of rewards, your creative approaches are likely to feel much more rewarding and easier to sustain over time.

8. *Shape environments that will support your creativity.* Find friends who will recognize your distinctiveness. Choose a major in which your individuality can shine. Avoid work environments that feel oppressive, mechanical, or uninspired.

9. *Actively pursue the creative life.* If you accept the proposition that you are not creative, then you won't be. If you open yourself to maximizing your creative potential, you begin the journey.

Applying the Six Strategies for Success

How does the material in this chapter make you think about ways you can succeed in college, particularly in terms of your thinking processes? Write down your personal insights from reading the chapter that help you make meaningful links to the six strategies for success described on page 31.

Putting It All Together

1. List three things that distinguish good critical thinkers from bad ones. Do these characteristics apply to you? If not, how can you improve your critical thinking skills?

2. Write down a question you have about something you are currently studying. Is it a "good" question based on what you have read in this chapter? Analyze why or why not.

3. List some steps you can take now to improve your creativity. How can this help you achieve "flow"?

4. In your journal or on paper, write about an important decision you made that was very satisfying to you. For example, did you select the right college to begin your academic career? What about the process helped to ensure that your decision would be right? What aspects of this process can you practice regularly in making sound decisions in the future?

5 › Take Effective Notes

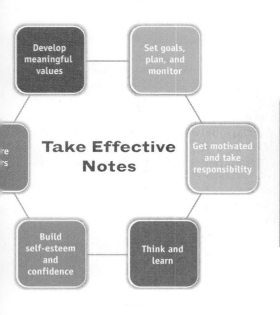

Take Effective Notes

Develop meaningful values

Set goals, plan, and monitor

Get motivated and take responsibility

Think and learn

Build self-esteem and confidence

Motivate yourself by adopting helpful strategies to select, think about, and learn new ideas that college has to offer. As you read, think about the "Six Strategies for Success" listed to the left and how this chapter can help you maximize success in these important areas, particularly "Think and Learn."

Commit

Some classes will be exciting from start to finish. You'll look forward to these lectures and linger after each. It's easy to follow through on your commitment to learning when courses match your learning style or personal interest. When the content of the class or the style of the lecturer is not a good match, making a strong commitment to attend class is even more important. Before each class, get ready to learn.

Anticipate Review your notes from the last class as well as your reading assignment. Identify any areas that are difficult to understand, and think about questions that could clarify them. Or search the web to find other sources that might clarify these areas. Read your syllabus to determine the topics for discussion in class, and make sure you have done any reading associated with these lecture topics.

Be on Time Even better, arrive a few minutes early. This gives you a chance to review your notes before class, and be ready to go as soon as the instructor begins. Well organized instructors often use the first few minutes of class to review the previous class. This allows you to rehearse what you've been learning. Like reviewing your notes, it also sets the stage for how the upcoming class will unfold, which will help you get organized and figure out what's most important.

Don't Miss Classes The best way to be prepared is to attend all your classes. Even if you haven't done the assigned reading, the class will still be worthwhile. The lecture may be so fascinating that it makes it easier to sit down and do a double dose of reading in preparation for the next class. If you can't attend class, use good judgment about how to compensate.

Do the Assignments Assignments aren't usually optional. Instructors design assignments to help students develop expertise in the content and skills that the course has to offer. From the outset of the class, plan how to complete all of your assignments to get the most from your courses.

Some students assume that reading assignments aren't all that important because the instructor will cover the material in class. This is not a wise assumption. Many instructors assign readings as a related but independent resource; they do not review them. Successful students complete assigned readings *before* class to better understand the lecture. Connections and overlaps between the lecture and readings reinforce learning. Another reason to complete reading assignments is that you may be called on to report your impressions. It's embarrassing when you haven't got a clue what to say.

Concentrate

Many things influence concentration. For example, if you're an auditory learner or have a natural interest in the topic, extracting what you need from a lecture may not be hard. Other circumstances, though, will require you to take a more strategic approach to concentration.

Minimize Distractions You can do many things to minimize distractions:

1. *Sit near the front.* If you can't see or hear clearly, find a spot where you can.

2. *Reduce noise.* The instructor may not realize how noisy the room is for you, so do what you need to ensure your best hearing. Close doors and windows to reduce unwanted noise. Move away from chatty neighbors.

3. *Reduce off-task pressures.* Get the sleep you need, and eat before class to quiet a growling stomach. If a specific worry keeps bothering you, write it down separately from your notes. Promise yourself that you'll worry about it later, so you can let it go for now.

4. *Stay tuned in.* If something in the lecture distresses you—either content or delivery style—concentrate on identifying more precisely what bothers you and how you can best resolve the problem. Focus on hearing what you most likely will be tested on. Breathe deeply and use other stress management techniques to stay in tune.

5. *Track your progress.* Keep records of how much time you spend paying attention. At the end of each class, estimate what percentage of time you were on track and write the figure in the upper right-hand corner of your notes. Try to make regular improvements in your rate. Instructors differ in their ability to lecture.

Listen Actively To succeed you need to concentrate. One way to do this is to listen actively. Active listeners sort through the information they hear and figure out what's most important. They connect what they hear with things they already know. Although it's hard work, active listening is an efficient way to get the most from a lecture.

In contrast, passive listeners merely write down the instructor's words without necessarily understanding the ideas or making judgments about their importance. Unfortunately, putting understanding off until later not only makes ideas harder to learn, it also takes time from preparations for the next assignment.

Capture Key Messages

Since every lecture or discussion is different, you will have to be flexible in your note-taking strategies. You may need to experiment in each class until you find just the right note-taking groove. What are some strategies you can use to recognize key points?

Identify Key Words, Themes, and Main Points Often these are ideas that the instructor repeats, highlights, illustrates with examples, supports with related facts, or displays on a blackboard or screen.

Most instructors organize courses around a central set of terms. Recognizing broader themes may be more challenging. Sometimes your instructor will give you an overarching theme to help you organize what you're about to hear. If the instructor does not, make a point to think about what theme the details of the lecture suggest and how they relate to themes from previous lectures. Try to keep the big picture in mind so you don't feel overwhelmed by the details.

Recognize Organization Patterns in the Lecture Listen for some key words that will signal patterns—how main points and supporting details relate. This anticipation will help you to grasp the logic and flow of the lecture and minimize the tendency to get lost in details and digressions. Some examples of such patterns include:

- *Listing Patterns:* All of the relevant facts, concepts, and events are presented in simple lists that reflect order of importance. Signal words include *first, second, also, in addition, another, moreover, next, furthermore.*

- *Comparison Patterns:* This pattern focuses on similarities and differences. Signal words include *on one hand, similarly, in contrast, but, then, either, or, compared to, opposite of, like.*

- *Sequence Patterns:* Many times instructors will incorporate timelines, chronologies, or procedural steps or stages to show how things are fixed in a certain order. Signal words include *first, second, finally, while, now, then, next.*

- *Cycle Patterns:* Cycle patterns of organization show how trends end up where they started. Signal words include *first, second, finally, while, now, then, same, circular.*

- *Problem-Solving Patterns:* In this type of organization, the instructor identifies a problem, establishes conditions for solving the problem, explains the solution, and predicts the aftereffects. Signal words include *since, resulting, hypothesis, leading to, because, so, if . . . then, solution.*

- *Cause-Effect Patterns:* This pattern involves showing causal connections between two events. Signal words include *prediction, effect, causation, control.*

- *Example Patterns:* This pattern involves defining a concept and then offering examples or illustrations to clarify or explain the term. Signal words include *for example, for instance, other examples include, such as.*

Relate Details to the Main Point Instructors use stories, examples, or analogies to reinforce main points. They usually intend their stories to do more than entertain. Check to make sure you understand why the instructor chose a particular story or example. Pay attention to how much the instructor relies on important de-

Recognizing patterns in your instructors' lectures helps you organize your notes.

Tackling Tough Lectures

The fast-talking lecturer

Enthusiastic instructors may talk too fast for you to catch what they're saying. When you're confronted with a fast talker:

Ask the instructor politely to slow down.

Encourage the instructor to write the key terms on the board or on a handout.

Focus on the major thrust, not the detail.

The bewildering lecturer

Some instructors simply use more sophisticated language than you may be used to hearing. When your instructor is hard to understand:

Prepare for class carefully by doing all assigned reading.

Ask for restatements.

Try to appreciate the increase you are getting in your vocabulary.

The disorganized lecturer

Some lecturers organize poorly. They go off on tangents or don't teach from an organized plan. If you have a chaotic instructor:

Look at the big picture, concentrating on larger themes.

Form a study group to help make sense of it.

Impose organization using note-taking strategies.

The tedious lecturer

Instructors give boring lectures because they have lost interest in their work or don't understand classroom dynamics well. Some instructors even suffer from stage fright. If you have a boring instructor:

Make connections between what the instructor is saying and what you already know.

Ask questions that encourage examples.

Show active interest in the lecture.

---

tails at test time. Some instructors may expect you to be accountable for all of the details. Others will emphasize your ability to communicate your understanding of the main ideas with the most important details.

Listen for Clues Pay special attention to words that signal a change of direction or special emphasis. For example, note when a concept or topic comes up more than once. Such a topic is likely to show up on an exam. Transition speech, such as "in contrast to" or "let's move on to" or even "this will be on the next exam," signals the change of topics or the emergence of new key points. Lists usually signify important material that is also easy to test. Instructors are most likely to test for ideas that they consider exciting, so listen for any special enthusiasm.

Work on Your "Sixth Sense" Some students just know when an instructor is covering key ideas, especially material that's likely to be on the test. They sit, pencils poised, and wait for the instructor to get to the good stuff. Actively categorize what your instructor is saying by asking questions such as: Is this statement central to my understanding of today's topic? Does this example help clarify the main ideas? Is this a tangent (an aside) that may not help me learn the central ideas?

Save Your Energy Don't write down what you already know. Besides covering new material, lectures usually overlap some with material in required textbooks. If you have read your assignment, you should be able to recognize when the lecture overlaps the text. Open your text and follow along, making notes in the margins where the instructor stays close to the text. Pay closer attention when what you hear sounds unfamiliar.

Connect Ideas

The best listeners don't just check in with the speaker from time to time. They work at listening by using strategies to create more enduring impressions of the lecture and to escape daydreaming.

Paraphrase What You Hear If you can't translate the ideas from a lecture into your own words, you may need to do more reading or ask more questions until you are able to do so.

Relate Key Ideas to What You Already Know When you can see how the course ideas connect to other aspects of your life, including your experiences in other courses or to contemporary events, the ideas will be easier to remember. For example, if you're studying in sociology how societies organize into different economic classes, think about how those ideas apply to the neighborhood where you grew up.

Make a Note of Unknown Words Sometimes unknown words are a signal that you've missed something in a previous lecture. If you take notes on a laptop, you may be able to look up meanings in an electronic dictionary as you go. Consider making a computer file to store these terms for easy review. If not, write the word at the top of your notes and look it up right after class. Keep a running list of the words that gave you trouble. Your list becomes a natural tool for review before exams.

Own Your Confusion It's inevitable. Sometimes you will be confused. The instructor may use terms you don't understand or present relationships that may be too subtle to grasp the first time you hear them. If English is your second language, there may be other reasons why you lose your way. The instructor may speak too fast for you to process the information. Clearly mark your notes with a question mark or other code that identifies the area as one you need to revisit. Make a point to confer with classmates, check on the Internet, explore your text for backup support, or even talk with the instructor after class until you get back on the right path.

Get Involved When you determine the direction that the class will take, you can come up with examples that make ideas more compelling. Suggest those examples to the instructor. Say, "Would this be an example of what you are talking about?" Ask questions. Answer questions when the instructor asks them. Participate in discussions that are prompted by the lecture. No matter what form your involvement takes, it will help you stay engaged with the ideas in the lecture.

Master Note-Taking Strategies

You'll learn a great deal by taking careful notes. In addition to always writing down the class, title or topic of lecture, your name, and e-mail address, always use the following strategies:

Reduce to Key Ideas Simplify what you record from lectures to the fewest words possible in order to capture the key ideas. Shorter notes will help you concentrate on the most critical details.

Take Notes from All Relevant Input Some students believe that only the instructor's input is worth recording. However, you may be tested on information that other students present, as well as videos or films that are shown in class.

Don't Erase Mistakes Erasing an error takes more time than simply crossing out. Not erasing also lets you restore the information later, if need be.

Use Abbreviations Use standard abbreviations to record information quickly. Develop your own abbreviations for words that you need to write often. When instructors use terms regularly throughout the course, develop abbreviations for them as well. For example, *EV* might stand for *evolution* or *A/R* for *accounts receivable*. When you use personalized abbreviations, write their meanings inside the cover of your notebook as a handy reference.

Review Your Notes Often Whenever possible, review your notes right after class. Some students like to rewrite or type up their notes after class as a way of consolidating information. If you don't rewrite, at least reread your notes to add whatever might be missing. Highlight certain phrases, identify the key points, or revise notes that are unclear. Review your notes between classes to consolidate your learning and again just before the next class meeting.

Tape Lectures Selectively Some students like to tape lectures as a backup for the notes, but it isn't always a good idea. Tape the lecture only if you must be absent, you have a learning disability that hinders listening carefully or accurately, or you foresee the need for the complete text of a lecture likely to be dense or complex.

Organize Your Materials for Easy Retrieval A separate notebook or compartment in a binder for each subject can improve your efficiency. Three-ring binders allow you to rearrange and add pages. Write on only one side of the page to make your notes easy to arrange and review later. Some students, especially tactile learners, use index cards because they're easy to carry, organize, and review.

Request Feedback about Your Notes If you struggle with note taking, ask your instructor for help during an office hours visit. Ask whether you are capturing the main ideas in your notes; if not, discuss ways to improve your note taking.

Evaluate Your Note-Taking Strategy When you get a test back, examine the structure of your notes to see what accounted for your success. Continue to practice the strategies that served you well. Modify practices that may have made it hard for you to learn or test well.

Take Great Lecture Notes

Taking great notes is your opportunity to think and learn actively during your time in class. With proper planning and monitoring, great notes will cut your review time and help consolidate your learning. You have numerous good options for taking notes. Choose one that suits your learning needs and preferences.

Summary Method Summarizing appeals most to students with auditory learning preferences. They are comfortable in the world of words and have learned to trust that they can extract the key ideas after the fact. Writing summaries helps you take responsibility for judging what is crucial and relating that to other aspects of the course. It's also an effective way to handle a disorganized lecturer. With the summary method, however, you run the risk that some key ideas might be overlooked.

Outlining An outline summarizes key points and subpoints. The Links to Success lists at the beginning of each chapter of this book are one example of an outline. When you use an outline form, the results are neat and well organized. Naturally, outlines are easiest to create when the lecture itself is well organized.

You can outline using numbers or letters, or you can simply use indentations to signify subpoints. The distinctiveness of an outline appeals to students who are especially good at analysis and critical thinking. The outline shows the relationship among ideas and reduces the lecture to its key points, showcased by a systematic visual display that can be easier for visual than auditory learners. Outlining will sharpen critical thinking skills because, when done properly, it provides practice in analyzing the course content.

The Cornell System Choose the Cornell method if you demonstrate a preference for auditory learning and show conscientiousness about review. To use the Cornell method, draw a vertical line down your loose-leaf or notebook page about 2 ½ inches from the left edge of the page. Draw a horizontal line across the page about two inches from the bottom. Use the largest area on the right side of the page to take your notes during class. After class is over, use the blank left side of the page to write short headings or questions for each part of your notes. Use the bottom of the page for a summary or other comments and questions.

The Cornell system creates a great tool for reviewing. Cover up the right-hand portion of the page and use the phrases or questions on the left side as prompts. As you read each prompt, practice recalling the details on the right. The Cornell method can also be combined with summarizing or outlining to take advantage of the strengths of those approaches.

Concept Maps A concept map provides visual cues about how ideas are related. Some students construct concept maps during class from lecture notes. Others may draw concept maps after class as a way to review the material. Concept mapping appeals to visual learners with a creative flair. Concept maps are more engaging to create and facilitate recall better than other formats for visual learners. Here is an example of a concept map:

Figure 5.1 The Cornell Method The Cornell method separates running notes taken during class from summary phrases and an overall summary or comments added after class. To review, cover the material on the right and practice recalling it from the cues on the left.

Dr. King -- Psychology 21   Tues. 9-14-02
Topic: Optimism & Pessimism -- Seligman's theory

Success:
2 keys or 3?

Talent and desire, 2 keys to success. Is there a 3rd key --
"optimism"? (=expecting to succeed)? The real test=how you
react when something bad happens. Give up or fight on?

Lab studies on
learning/unlearning
helplessness

Psych lab experiments can teach dogs to be helpless. If dog is
trained to think it has no control over when it will get shocked, it
starts acting helpless even when it could jump away & not get
shocked. Same type thing happens to people in childhood. If they
don't think they can change things, they act helpless: pessimistic.
But you can also train a dog out of being helpless. All depends
on expecting to be or not be in control.
How optimists vs. pessimists explain bad events.

Pessimist:

"P P P"

1. Personal -- "Bad things are my fault."
2. Permanent -- "Can't get better."
3. Pervasive -- "Affects everything I do."

Optimist:
1. Impersonal -- "Bad things not my fault."
2. Momentary -- "Can change tomorrow."
3. Particular -- "Doesn't affect the rest of me."

Pessimism →
depression

Everyone can get depressed, but pessimists stay depressed longer.
Why? Because of how they explain things.

Therapy = Change
explanations

Cognitive therapy: Change the way pessimist explains things to cure
their depression. How? First get them to hear what they tell
themselves when things go bad. Then get them to change what they
say.

Seligman found that desire and talent don't always win. Optimism also important.
Pessimists can become "helpless" in hard times. Optimists recover faster. Training
pessimists to think more optimistically might reduce depression.
Q: But how does it work? Find out Thursday!

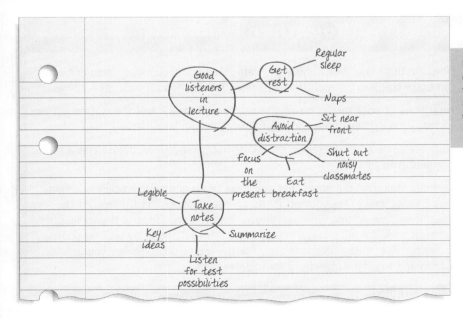

Figure 5.2 The Concept Map A concept map is a helpful tool for visual learners. It displays the key ideas in a lecture or resource and shows how the ideas relate to each other.

Take Notes on Your Reading

The expertise you develop in taking good notes during lectures can also help you take effective notes from reading assignments. The principles are the same: Capture the main ideas, show how secondary information connects and supports main ideas, and choose a note-taking format that maximizes your retention and learning.

Choose a Sound Strategy

- *Use a highlighter to identify crucial ideas.*
- *Add personal notes in the margins to enhance meaning.*
- *Create a set of external notes.*
- *Translate the source carefully into your own words.*
- *Avoid writing things down that you don't understand.*
- *Transform the text into pictures, tables, or diagrams.*
- *Periodically evaluate the quality of your notes.*

Applying the Six Strategies for Success

How does the material in this chapter make you think about ways you can succeed in college, particularly in terms of your note-taking techniques? Write down your personal insights from reading the chapter that help you make meaningful links to the six strategies for success described on page 41.

Putting It All Together

1. What are three tips for listening most effectively to challenging lectures? How can these tips also be applied to absorbing information for difficult readings?

2. What style of note taking makes the most sense for each of the classes you're currently taking? List your classes, followed by the best method.

3. What are some good strategies for taking notes on your readings? List a few pros and cons of each.

4. Carefully look over the notes that you have taken in a course where learning isn't coming easily. Ask yourself if you are staying tuned in throughout the class, if you are writing down words you don't understand, and if your lecture notes fit with the big picture. Follow up on your reflection by visiting your instructor. Take your notes with you. Ask the instructor to review your approach and to offer suggestions for improvement.

6 > Read for Success

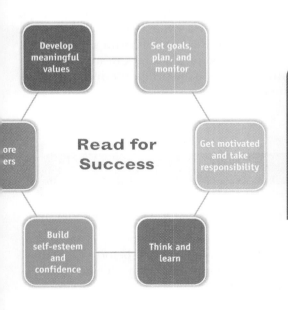

Read for Success

Develop meaningful values

Set goals, plan, and monitor

ore ers

Get motivated and take responsibility

Build self-esteem and confidence

Think and learn

You can become a better reader by using proven strategies. As you read this chapter, think about how the "Six Strategies for Success" listed to the left can help you maximize success in these important areas, particularly "Think and Learn."

Create a Good Reading Environment

Because college reading takes concentration, it's important to create an environment that lets you focus on your assignments. That environment includes both the physical setting in which you read and your attitude toward your reading goals.

Plan Time and Space to Concentrate

Schedule blocks of time for reading in a place where you won't be interrupted. On your main schedule, set aside times for study. Clear other concerns from your mind so you can concentrate.

Students differ about where they prefer to read. Many like the library. Others find it *too* quiet or full of distracting people. Try a few settings to find out which ones work best for you. If you can spend only a little time on campus, you may face particular challenges in securing quiet space and uninterrupted time. Some commuters on public transportation can read and review while they travel. If you're stuck with reading an assignment in a noisy environment, you may want to wear headphones with familiar instrumental music just loud enough to block distractions. If you have a long drive to school, you can listen to taped classes.

If you have to combine reading with child care, plan to read during nap times, after the children have gone to bed, or before they get up. Or set a timer for 15 minutes and provide activities that your children can do at the table with you. Let them know that at the end of 15 minutes—when the timer goes off—everyone will take a play break. If possible, find other students with similar child-care needs. Pool your resources to hire a regular baby-sitter or trade baby-sitting services to free up more time for reading.

Create a Good Mental Environment

Attitude and commitment have a lot to do with reading well. These additional strategies will help you improve your reading skills.

- *Stay positive.* Keep a positive attitude. Others have succeeded before you. If they could manage, so can you. If you approach your reading with a feeling of defeat, you may give up instead of pulling through.

- *Make the author your companion.* Most authors envision themselves talking to their readers as they write. As you read, imagine talking to the author as a way of making your reading more lively. When you approach reading as one end of a conversation, it may be easier to make comments, to see relationships, and to be critical.

- *Pace yourself according to the difficulty level.* When you're naturally drawn to a reading or it fits in well with your abilities or interests, you may not have to struggle to get the key ideas. However, you may need to read some difficult writing three or four times before it begins to make sense. When you have two or more kinds of reading to complete, read the harder or duller one first, while your concentration is strongest.

- *Take breaks.* How long you can read between breaks depends on how hard you have to work to grasp the ideas. Examine the material to see whether there are natural breaks, such as the ends of sections, that correspond to your attention span. When you've completed each reading goal, reward yourself with a walk, a brief visit with someone, or some pleasure reading.

- *Shift gears when you do not make progress.* A fresh start may be required if you find yourself reading and rereading the same passage. Try writing notes on the reading. Take a break. Get something to drink. Call a classmate to confer about your struggle. Return to the passage with an intention to read more slowly until the clouds part.

- *Find other sources if the reading is confusing.* Sometimes an author's style is hard to comprehend. For nonfiction, find a clearer book on the same topic at the library or bookstore. Make sure that it covers material similar to your assigned test. Browsing the Internet may be helpful as well. Some bookstores sell guides to certain disciplines that may help to clarify basic ideas. Keep your introductory textbooks as references for when you are challenged in later, tougher courses. Get help from an instructor or tutor in finding other sources.

- *Build your vocabulary.* College is a great place to expand your vocabulary. In the process of learning the specialized languages in a discipline, you'll also expand your general vocabulary. Get a dictionary or use the electronic version on your computer to look up words you don't know. Keep a list of new words and their meanings on an index card to use as a bookmark or in an electronic file on your computer.

- *Work on reading faster.* Fast readers tend to be more effective learners than slow readers, not only because they remember more of what they read but also because they save valuable time (Armstrong & Lampe, 1990). Improve your reading speed by concentrating on processing more words with each sweep of your eyes across a line of text. For example, if you normally scan three words at a time, practice taking in four words with each scan or scan to read whole phrases instead of individual words. You can also ask to have your reading abilities tested formally by reading specialists at the college. They can help you identify specific problems and solutions.

- *Set goals.* Make commitments that will help you feel more responsible for what you've read. Join a study group or promise to tutor another student who needs help. Some students consult with their instructors about how best to contribute to class on a given day. This strategy is especially helpful for shy students.

Capture and Connect Ideas

A good reading system includes some of the following types of reading: previewing, skimming, active reading, analytic reading, and reviewing.

Before You Read It is always a good idea to preview the material before you sit down to read. This helps you estimate how intense your reading effort will need to be and how much time it will take to complete the assignment. It also gives you a broad overview of the material that can make it easier to understand and remember the details.

Preview the reading. What is the context for the assignment? What have you been doing in class that led up to this reading assignment? Think about the length of the reading and estimate how long it will take to read the assignment. Look at the structure and features of the reading. Find the section endings so that you can plan when to take a break. How difficult is the reading? Higher-level material may require more than one reading.

While You Read You can read at several different levels, depending on the difficulty and importance of the material and the time you have to devote to the task. *Skimming* covers the content at a general level. When you skim, you read at about twice your average rate. To skim, focus on introductory statements, topic sentences (usually the first sentence in the paragraph), and boldface terms. Slow down to examine summaries carefully. Make sure you understand the points that the author intends.

You don't always need to read every word of every assignment (Frank, 1996). Your ability to read selectively improves as you grow accustomed to how readings relate to a course and how your instructor chooses test material. Skimming provides you with the surface structure of the ideas in the text, when that is all you have time for. Successful skimmers can usually participate in class discussions with some confidence if they rehearse the main ideas and have read some key passages.

Active reading prevents the wasted time of empty reading—that type of reading where your eyes track across the lines of text but your brain fails to register anything meaningful. Immerse yourself in what the author is trying to say. Identify the main ideas and understand how the supporting points reinforce those ideas. Also construct the meaning in what you read by linking the information to your own personal knowledge or experience. Use these questions as guidelines for active reading:

Have I ever experienced anything similar to what is described in the reading?

How does this relate to things I already know?

How might this be useful for me to know?

Do I like or agree with these ideas?

How does the reading relate to current events?

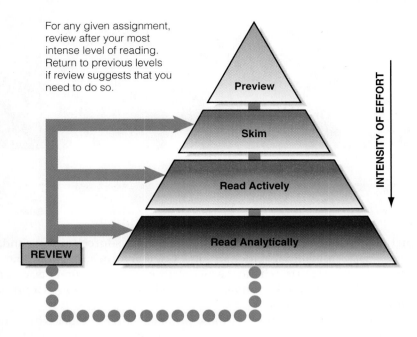

For any given assignment, review after your most intense level of reading. Return to previous levels if review suggests that you need to do so.

Active readers form as many links as possible between their personal experience and knowledge and what they're reading.

Analytic reading requires questioning both the author and yourself as you dig through a reading. The following questions may help you become an analytic reader:

What are the author's values and background? Do these influence the writing? How?

Does the author's bias taint the truthfulness of what I'm reading?

What implicit (unstated) assumptions does the author make?

Do I believe the evidence?

Is the author's position valid?

Are the arguments logically developed?

What predictions follow from the argument?

What are the strengths and weaknesses of the argument?

Is anything missing from the position?

What questions would I want to ask the author?

Is there a different way to look at the facts or ideas?

Would these ideas apply to all people in all cultures or in all situations?

After You Read The final step in a successful reading plan is to review the material after it has been read. There are several different strategies for reviewing.

Reviewing is an opportunity to test yourself on your own comprehension. Question yourself on details or write out summaries of what you've read. The quality of your notes can make all the difference when it's time to study for a test. With well constructed notes that you have reviewed systematically after your classes, your final review should be a breeze.

Read for Success in All of Your Courses

Primary and Secondary Sources

The two general types of readings for courses are primary sources and secondary sources. A *primary source* is material written in some original form such as autobiographies, speeches, research reports, scholarly articles, government documents, and historical journal articles. For example, you may read the U.S. Constitution as a primary source in your political science class.

Secondary sources summarize or interpret these primary sources. A magazine article that discussed politicians' interpretations of the Constitution generally would be considered a secondary source. Textbooks are secondary sources that try to give a comprehensive view of information from numerous primary works.

You have many more opportunities to read primary sources in college than you did in high school. Most people find reading original works exhilarating. For example, reading a speech by Frederick Douglass about the abolition of slavery will likely stimulate you more than reading interpretations of his speeches. Primary sources may be more difficult to read than secondary sources, however, because a secondary source often summarizes and interprets the meaning of the primary source. Original works must be chewed and digested; secondary sources do some of the chewing and digesting for you.

Interpreting original ideas is also more challenging than accepting others' interpretations. When reading primary sources, learn as much as you can about the intentions of the authors and the historical context in which they were writing. Understanding a historical period will help you interpret texts written at that time.

Reading in Different Disciplines

As you've already discovered, some readings are harder than others for you. Obviously, you'll learn material more easily if it matches an area in which you have special interests and intellectual strengths. However, liberal arts programs almost always require reading about topics that don't come naturally. In some readings, technical terms may slow you down. Other readings may require more imagination. Let's explore some tips that will help you read more efficiently in a variety of disciplines, some of which will be more challenging for you than others.

Literature In literature courses, you study poetry, novels, plays, and short stories. Appreciation of these forms comes most easily to people who enjoy reflective learning and who like to think critically. For them, many great works provide delight. But what strategies can help you when reading literature is challenging?

- *Use your imagination.* Visualize the action. Participate at the level the author intended: Use as many senses as the author used—taste, smell, sound—as you recreate the author's world in your imagination.

- *Look for connections.* Are any of the experiences like your own? Do the characters remind you of anyone you know?

- *Make the author real.* Search the Internet for a good biography or for personal details about the author that might help you understand the author's motivation to create the work.
- *Make a chart.* If the reading is complex, make a list of key figures as they are introduced so you can easily review it as the story progresses.
- *Predict what will happen.* Once you understand the direction the work is taking, see if you can anticipate what happens next.
- *Read aloud.* Some great works are savored best when read aloud. Find a study partner and share the task.

Visualizing a work of literature the way the author intended it to be performed can help you understand and enjoy it.

History Some students love history because they believe that we are all the walking expression of history. History texts provide a great opportunity to use your imagination and it will come alive if you let it. Good readers in history put conscientious effort into seeing how events, places, and people interconnect.

- *Put yourself in the picture.* As you read about events, think about how you might have reacted to them at the time.
- *Change history.* Predict an alternative course of history by changing a critical event or two. How might the ripple effect have changed some element of your life?
- *Imagine or draw the timeline.* Articulate a causal link from one event to the next over time.
- *Make it into a movie.* Imagine a cast of film stars in the roles of the historical figures you're reading about. It may help you visualize the action better.
- *Don't forget the big picture.* Keep in mind how each new event or person you encounter in your learning adds to your understanding of the grander historic scale.

Natural and Social Science The terminology presented in the sciences represents a kind of shorthand that allows scientists to communicate with each other. Learning these terms can be a challenge without some helpful strategies.

- *Keep a running glossary of terms or use the glossary in your textbook, if there is one.* Treat the sciences like a foreign language. Study the meaning of each new term.
- *Accept the role of numbers.* If you aren't comfortable with numbers, you may be turned off by the level of measurement and statistics that pervades most sciences. When numbers accompany text, spend extra time understanding their significance.
- *Think practically.* See if you can come up with a practical application of the scientific relationships you're reading about.
- *Look for links in the news.* The sciences regularly issue progress reports that may enhance your understanding or clarify concepts.
- *Cruise the Internet.* Chances are good that the Internet will provide ideas that will help you with the terms. Find information about the scientists themselves that will help make the enterprise feel more real to you.
- *Look for overlaps.* Where does your life intersect with the scientific ideas you're trying to learn?

making connections — Reading Strategies for Different Situations

- When you want to develop understanding of the ideas:
  Preview → Active reading → Review
- When you want to practice critical thinking about your reading:
  Preview → Analytic reading → Review
- When you have trouble retaining what you read:
  Preview → Skim → Active reading → Review → Review
- When you don't have time to read for mastery:
  Skim → Review (pay close attention to summaries and boldface terms)

Improve Your Memory

Short-term and Long-term Memory

You will spend a substantial amount of time in college committing important facts, ideas, and theories to memory. Memorizing is a fundamental skill that expands your knowledge base and lays a foundation for more sophisticated thinking skills as you learn about different disciplines. Two important memory systems are involved in academic learning: *short-term memory* and *long-term memory*.

Short-Term Memory Short-term memory ("working memory") enables us to get some work done without cluttering up our minds. For example, when you look up a new phone number, it doesn't automatically go into your long-term memory for important numbers. Short-term memory lets you retain it briefly, for 30 seconds or so, just long enough to get the number dialed. Then it vanishes.

Besides being brief, short-term memory has limited capacity. It can hold approximately seven "chunks" of information before the system becomes overtaxed and information is dumped out of awareness (Miller, 1956).

You may be able to trick short-term memory into holding more detail through a process called *chunking:* making each "memory chunk" represent more than one piece of information. This is the basis for *mnemonics*, or memory aids, discussed later.

Long-Term Memory You've already stored a mountain of facts and impressions in your long-term memory from your education and life experience. Each memory exists in your long-term memory. Ideally, you can *retrieve* it as needed.

Unfortunately, no matter how hard you study, you're bound to forget some things you learn. The two main reasons why we forget, are *interference* and *decay*. Interference can crowd out memories, making them difficult to retrieve. For example, when you take a full course load, the sheer volume of the material may cause interference among the subjects, especially when courses use similar terms for different purposes. Memory decay occurs when we fail to review regularly or do not practice retrieving information. As a result, you may find it impossible to recall a piece of information when you want it, such as during a test. This is why it is important to regularly review what you have learned.

How to Memorize

The best way to make long-term memories is through understanding.

Pay Close Attention Don't allow yourself to be distracted when you're processing information about things you must do or remember. Some absentmindedness is caused by failing to absorb the information in the first place.

Concentrate on one thing at a time. You may have to study multiple subjects in one session. If so, try to focus your attention on the subject at hand. Study the most difficult subjects first because you need more energy for harder material. Reward yourself at the end by saving the subject you enjoy most for last.

If you're taking two similar subjects, they may offer overlapping or conflicting ideas. To keep the ideas separate in your mind and reduce the amount of interference between them, space these subjects apart when you study. If you must study for multiple tests in a short time frame, schedule your final study session in a particular subject as the last thing you do before the test.

Involve Yourself in Your Studies Look for personal connections. This will make it easier to learn and recall unfamiliar or abstract ideas (Matlin, 1998), especially if you're a visual learner. Ask yourself questions about what you've read or what you've recorded about class activities. Expand the number of associations you make with the information.

Create Memory Prompts Organize concepts in a tree diagram or concept map to provide additional cues for remembering ideas. For example, suppose you're studying important events in U.S. history in the 1950s. Construct a map that captures the important, related details of the period to make them easier to remember.

Use Mnemonics Mnemonics (ne-mon-ix) are strategies that expand visual or auditory associations and help you learn. They involve linking something you want to remember to images, letters, or words that you already know or that are easy to recall because of how you've constructed the mnemonic. They can be visual or text-based, logical or goofy, complex or simple. For instance, you can recall the nine planets (Mercury, Venus, Earth, Mars, Jupiter, Saturn, Uranus, Neptune, Pluto) in order using the phrase My Very Elegant Mother Just Served Us Nine Pickles.

Use Props Create a set of flash cards or audiotapes and carry them with you. Rehearse while you wait in a grocery store line, at the laundromat, or at the doctor's office.

Construct a "Cram Card" Whenever you can't commit important information to long-term memory through regular study and rehearsal, write down the essential points on a small card (Frank, 1996). Study the card before your test, up to the point when your instructor says to put materials away.

Overlearn When you think that you really know your stuff, study just a bit longer to "overlearn" the material.

Exploit Situational Cues If you can, when you take an exam, sit in the seat you normally sit in for class. Being in the same place may help you dredge up memories that might be hard to remember without context cues.

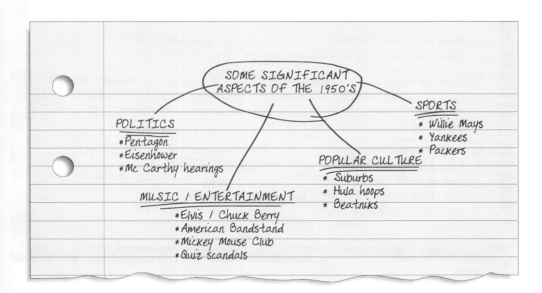

Use images to improve your recall of important information.

Use Rhymes and Songs If you were raised in the United States, you may have learned when Columbus came to America through rhyme: "Columbus sailed the ocean blue/In fourteen hundred ninety-two." Melodies also can produce enduring memories. Many children learn their phone numbers or addresses when parents sing the information to them using a familiar melody.

Acronyms Acronyms are special words (or sentences) that you construct using the first letter from each word in the list you wish to memorize. The acronym cues you not only to the items on the list but also to their proper order. For example, you can remember the names of the Great Lakes by remembering *HOMES* (Huron, Ontario, Michigan, Erie, Superior).

Drawings or diagrams Adding images can make recalling details easier. Draw pictures of the comparisons that your instructor uses to clarify concepts. For example, if your psychology instructor describes Freud's view of the unconscious as similar to an iceberg, draw a large iceberg in the background of your notes. Drawings are especially helpful for visual learners.

Applying the Six Strategies for Success

How does the material in this chapter make you think about ways you can succeed in college, particularly in terms of your reading? Write down your personal insights from reading the chapter that help you make meaningful links to the six strategies for success described on page 51.

Putting It All Together

1. What are three different ways to process information as you read? How can each style help you succeed in your various college courses? What type do you currently use most often, and why?

2. What are some strategies you can use to overcome distractions or time limitations to improve your college reading?

3. Select one section from this book. Develop a mnemonic to remember the key points from that section. Write it down. Tomorrow, revisit the mnemonic you've written down and see if you can still remember the items it represents. Did it help?

4. What is something you frequently forget? It could be an important concept from one of your classes, a particular type of appointment, or where you left your keys. In your journal or on paper to turn in, list a few strategies from this chapter that might help you address this memory lapse.

7 > Study Effectively

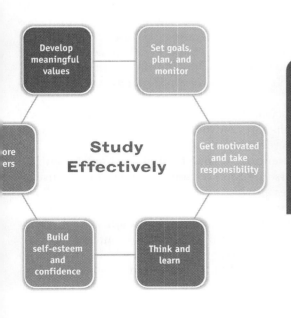

As you read, think about the "Six Strategies for Success" listed to the left and how this chapter can help you maximize success in these important areas. For example, effective study flows from solid planning based on your goals. Use these goals to motivate yourself to maximize your study skills and resources.

Plan Your Attack

Where to Study

Find the best place you can to work, and study there consistently. The best place is usually private, quiet, well lit, and comfortable in temperature. For many students, the best place will also involve access to a computer, including an online connection.

Narrow your study sites to one of a few places that provides you with the working space, storage space, and electronic access that will make your work efficient. You may find just the setup you need at home, in the library, at a dedicated purpose lab, within a residence hall, or even in a quiet but wired hallway somewhere on campus.

If you are a commuter, use your driving time to review audiotapes of complicated lectures, or carpool with someone in class to provide review time. Riding on a bus or train, especially if the commute is long, also provides blocks of study time and a chance to work online via a wireless network.

Wherever you study, minimize noise. Many people study best when the CD player, radio, and television are off. Some people like music in the background to mask other sounds and give a sense of control over the environment. If you can't control the noise around you, use headphones and soft instrumental music to minimize distraction.

When to Study

Allocate several hours outside class for every hour you spend in class. Outstanding students often put in even more time.

Review your notes immediately after class. This practice allows you to rehearse new ideas and identify unclear ones while they are fresh, so you can then clarify them with your instructor or in your reading. Reviewing your class notes and notes on reading assignments before the class meets again adds another rehearsal session that prepares you to participate in the next class more effectively. It also reinforces your memory on those concepts.

Know where, when, and how you study most effectively.

Also, schedule regular cumulative review sessions. If you regularly review your notes during the term, you'll need less review time right before exams.

Pay attention to your natural rhythms. If you're a night person, review sessions may be most effective after supper and late into the evening. If you're a morning person, you need to study earlier in the day to maximize your attention and concentration.

If you aren't getting the proper amount of rest, studying will be very difficult. You should be able to stay awake and alert if you have had sufficient sleep (Maas, 1998).

Stave off the Sleep Invasion

Use your desk *only* for studying.
When you drift asleep at your desk, you learn to associate your desk with napping, a cue you may not be able to afford.

Set an alarm.
Buy a wristwatch that can signal you at reasonable intervals to keep you focused.

Make a commitment to others.
Study with others and use the social contact to keep you from dozing off.

Take a five-minute fresh-air break.
A brisk walk can clear your mind so you can focus better when you return to your studies.

Stay involved in your reading.
The more invested you are, the less tempting it is to give in to sleepy feelings.

Get enough sleep to begin with.
You can manage a late night every once in a while, but a steady diet of all-nighters guarantees that you'll be fighting off the sandman.

What to Study

Use the daily and weekly calendar you established in Chapter 2 to decide when your activities must intensify or when you can take a much needed recreation break. Keep your long-term goals posted in your study area or use them as your computer screen saver so you can have easy access to reminders about what your commitments will require.

Set subgoals for each study session. Plan how long your study session will last as well as what specific tasks you want to accomplish and in what order. Build in some break time to help your concentration stay fresh. Monitor how well you're achieving these subgoals and adapt your planning and resources accordingly.

College instructors sometimes rely on a framework known as Bloom's Taxonomy that clarifies different kinds of learning and organizes them according to complexity. B. S. Bloom and his colleagues (1956) developed this hierarchy of cognitive skills to describe the kind of work that college courses require. Since then it has been modernized (Anderson & Krathwohl, 2001). The new taxonomy, like the original, is arranged from lower-order to higher-order cognitive skills.

- **Remember.** Retrieve pertinent acts from long-term memory *(recognize, recall)*.
- **Understand.** Construct new meaning by mixing new material with existing ideas *(interpret, exemplify, classify, summarize, infer, compare, explain)*.
- **Apply.** Use procedures to solve problems or complete tasks *(execute, implement)*.
- **Analyze.** Subdivide content into meaningful parts and relate the parts *(differentiate, organize, attribute)*.
- **Evaluate.** Come to a conclusion about something based on standards/criteria *(check, critique, judge)*.
- **Create.** Reorganize elements into a new pattern, structure, or purpose *(generate, plan, produce)*.
  [Source: Wilbert J. McKeachie, *Teaching Tips* Eleventh Edition, Houghton Mifflin Company, 2002.]

You can follow the spirit of Bloom's Taxonomy in your own approach to studying. Challenge yourself to go one level above what the course requires. For example, if your instructor emphasizes the learning of facts and figures in assignments, practice applying course materials to new situations. This emphasis will promote learning that endures.

Study for Each Subject

Courses differ in how much they make you think. You may have already noticed that you have to adjust your study strategies to different disciplines, especially when a subject isn't a great match for your learning style. However, you can apply this four-part framework to any subject to help you adjust to these differences and maximize your results:

- *The Rules.* Although each discipline requires memorizing new content, each also has sophisticated frameworks and theories that require deeper levels of thinking and understanding.
- *The Risks.* Each discipline tends to have special challenges associated with developing mastery.
- *The Resources.* Your learning style will make some disciplines more successful than others for you. Which elements of your learning style facilitate that success?
- *The Remedy.* If you're studying a discipline that doesn't match your learning style, you can take steps to improve your efficiency and effectiveness.

Natural Science and Math

The Rules Natural science and math are loaded with theorems, laws, and formulas that you'll probably need to memorize, but comprehension should be your primary objective. Most of the activities that you undertake in science and math provide practice in application; you apply the rules to produce a specific outcome or solution. Obviously, the more you practice applying the principles or formulas, the more enduring your learning will be.

The Risks Natural science and math often have an intimidating reputation. The stereotype is that only science and math "geeks" do well in these courses. It will help if you deflate your images about science slightly. For example, you regularly act like a scientist does when you figure out how things work, although you may not be as systematic or careful in your observations as scientists are. With some practice, you too, can do real science.

The Resources The natural sciences and mathematics attract students who have particular strengths in the logical-mathematical and naturalist dimensions of intelligence. Although the stereotype suggests that scientists do their work alone, progress in science depends on collaboration. Therefore, interpersonal intelligence also facilitates discovering and sharing new scientific knowledge.

Visual learners manage the challenges of mathematical formulas and also bring strong observational skills to science problems. Kinesthetic learners function well in laboratory exercises or field applications. Solving problems in natural science and mathematics also offers opportunities to exercise critical and creative thinking, thoughtful reflection, and active learning.

The Remedy If you don't have natural abilities to support your learning in the natural sciences and mathematics, try these strategies:

- Work through your preexisting assumptions. Understanding what you really know or think about a scientific event will help you see where your explanation may not be complete.

- Collaborate with others. This will help you improve your scientific problem solving.

- Change representational strategies. If the problem is presented graphically, translate the problem into text or vice versa.

- Keep the big picture in mind. What larger concepts are you mastering?

- Be persistent and check your work. Some problems don't yield a fast answer. Make sure your work is accurate before you turn it in.

- Try to relax. Seek counseling or tutoring if anxiety is getting in the way of your success.

The Humanities

The Rules Typically a humanities course is built around a particular *framework,* or set of concepts or theories, that will help you develop a new perspective or richer appreciation for the human condition. For example, learning about literature will expose you to various frameworks of literary criticism, such as psychoanalytic or feminist criticism. Each framework in turn is built on a distinct set of values and assumptions.

Applying the frameworks to literature will probably lead you to different kinds of conclusions. A psychoanalytic framework prompts you to look at unconscious motivations; a feminist framework sensitizes you to social forces that create different options for women and men. You can apply these frameworks to expand your personal insight. Humanities instructors look to your insights as evidence that you understand the frameworks.

The Risks You may fear that your personal interpretations will get you in trouble in humanities courses. You may assume that there is only one right answer and may be afraid that you'll look foolish if what you say is "wrong." However, the objective of most humanities courses is to encourage breadth of thinking. Take the risk of sharing your insights. You may end up offering ideas that your class members have never considered.

Notice that by using your imagination to think about your assignments, you also make new connections to the assigned material. The more connections you make, the easier it will be for you to recall information. This strategy also helps you anticipate and practice for essay tests.

The Resources Because of their learning styles, some students have a natural advantage in humanities courses.

- If you have verbal-linguistic intelligence, you bring a love of words and their meanings to complex humanities assignments.

- If you're skilled in auditory processing, you can track difficult lectures with ease.

- If you enjoy assignments that emphasize reflection and creative learning styles as well, humanities assignments offer you wide latitude for personal interpretation.

- If you like to think critically and creatively, you'll have many opportunities to create and defend your perspective.

The Remedy Not everyone has a learning style that makes learning in the humanities easy. What are some strategies you can use to enhance your success in humanities classes?

- *Keep a dictionary close.* You're bound to run into new terms that will slow down your reading.

- *Compare ideas.* Exploit any opportunity to discuss central ideas or identify challenging concepts.
- *Practice making conclusions.* Rehearse aloud or on paper the key ideas and principles you draw from the assignment.
- *Read to make connections.* The more you read about a topic, the more you'll have to reflect on.

Social Science

The Rules The social sciences produce laws and theories to explain the behavior of individuals and groups. Concepts in the social sciences often serve as shorthand for complex patterns of behavior. For example, *social stratification,* a sociological concept, refers to how people in a society can be classified into groups according to how much money they make, what types of jobs they have, how much power they wield, and so forth. Much of what students need to memorize in social science courses has to do with learning new terms such as stratification that explain human behavior.

The Risks Learning in the social sciences can be challenging because what you are expected to learn may conflict with what you previously believed. Say, for example, that you heard from your Uncle Ernie that it's dangerous to wake up a sleepwalker. It made sense to you, so you believe it. In your psychology class, however, you discover that this knowledge is inaccurate, and that it is more dangerous to allow a sleepwalker freedom to walk into trouble. You have to reject some things you thought were true—such as opinions from Uncle Ernie—to make room for new ideas derived from social science research.

Social scientists draw on multiple theories to explain the same thing. Social science is considered to be a "soft" science, because it has to explain many deeply complex problems that depend on numerous circumstances.

The Resources Both interpersonal and intrapersonal intelligence can help you understand the social part of social science. Logical-mathematical and naturalist intelligence support the science part of social science. Auditory and visual sensory styles help social scientists do what they do. The strong analytic requirements of social science tend to reward critical thinking, although other kinds of processing can also help.

The Remedy
- *Expect complexity.* You're less likely to be disappointed by the limits of social science if you understand that not all your questions will have clean answers. The most interesting topics are complex and do not present simple answers.
- *Use your own experience.* Most of the topics you'll study correspond to things you've already experienced. When you connect concepts to your experiences, you can bring additional associations that will make them easier to learn. However, don't restrict yourself to understanding only what you've personally experienced.
- *Stay open to alternative explanations.* Recognize that your experience may not be typical of the systematic observations in science. You'll need to practice staying objective as you evaluate evidence, which may include reevaluating the firm conclusions you have drawn from your personal experience.

Foreign Languages

The Rules The study of a foreign language is loaded with rules. Proper grammar, verb tenses, and noun forms such as "feminine" and "masculine" all represent rules that you must learn to acquire a new language. This may also include the norms and practices of the culture in which the language is practiced.

The Risks Many foreign languages have new sounds that may not be natural to you. You may fear revealing any shortcomings in your "ear" for language. The amount of time you have to spend drilling can also be daunting. Overcoming the risks and succeeding in foreign language classes involve understanding and memorizing as much as you can.

The Resources If you're blessed with a good ear for language, chances are good that you have a strong auditory sensory preference. Your fascination with words and meanings in another language point to verbal-linguistic intelligence. Because learning a new language requires a lot of memorization, the learning process of reflection may be the best tool available to help you learn a new language.

The Remedy

- *Use color-coded materials.* Color-coded flash cards may give you additional cues about the kinds of words you're trying to learn. For example, use blue cards for verbs, yellow for nouns, and so on.

- *Construct outrageous images.* Construct an image from the sounds of the language that will help you recall the vocabulary. For example, if you want to learn the word for "dinner" in Portuguese *(jantar)*, picture John eating a plate full of tar at the dinner table.

- *Talk out loud.* Label objects that you know. Rehearse routine conversations and stage practices with classmates when you can. Read your assignments aloud to improve your ear for the language.

- *Don't get behind.* Keep up, because this type of classwork will pile up fast.

- *Distribute your practice sessions.* Although using short but frequent study sessions to memorize college material is good in general, it's *essential* when you're learning a foreign language. Regular practice sessions make your learning last longer.

- *Immerse yourself.* Try to find some natural exposure to the language you're studying. Find a pen pal. Watch movies or television programs that feature the language you're studying.

Immerse yourself in the foreign language you are studying.

Join a Study Group

Working in a study group adds a vital element to your education and expands your resources. In addition to helping you better learn the course content, study groups can improve your ability to communicate, develop your project skills, and help you deal with conflict. How can you make group work most efficient and effective?

Don't wait for an instructor to convene a study group. Find interested and competent classmates to meet regularly and talk about a challenging course. Once you have made the commitment, stay the course. Some additional strategies include:

- Identify the hardest concepts or ideas you've encountered.
- Talk about the problems or ideas you especially like or dislike.
- Discuss which parts of the readings interest you the most.
- Help one another share and clarify everyone's understanding of the material.
- Discuss strategies for remembering course material.
- Generate questions to prepare for tests.
- Keep your commitments.

Whether the group is working on a 10-minute discussion project in class or a challenge that spans several weeks, effective groups usually work in stages such as the following:

1. *Plan the task.* As the group convenes, lay the groundwork for working together efficiently by doing four things:
   - Introduce group members. ("Who are we?")
   - Identify the purpose of meeting by agreeing on goals and objectives. ("What tasks do we need to do?")
       - Create a plan for working together. ("How can we work together efficiently?")
       - Set criteria for success. ("How will we know we've succeeded in our task?")

2. *Come to a consensus.* Once the ground rules have been established, your group can address the specific task at hand. You don't have to choose a formal leader, although that might be helpful. Group members who ask questions and move the group along help through informal guidance.

3. *Evaluate the results.* In the final stage of the discussion, summarize what has been accomplished and evaluate how well the group has performed so you can improve its efficiency. Then, plan your next meeting.

Group work can provide some of your most exciting—and most frustrating—learning. When you join others to solve a problem or explore the meaning of a work of art, your pooled brainpower can result in insights you might never have had on your own. Effective groups tend to bring out the best in their members.

Overcome Learning Disabilities

Nearly 1 in 10 people in the United States experiences complications in learning caused by a learning disability. Learning disabilities can interfere with incoming information by scrambling printed words, garbling spoken words, or causing confusion regarding numbers. As a result of confused input, people experience problems in expression, including impaired short-term memory, problematic spelling, confusion about terminology, substandard grammar, and poor math skills.

Clearly, students with learning disabilities face daunting problems, including some unfounded prejudices from professors and students who equate learning disability with low intelligence. However, many people with learning disabilities find great success in school and afterward in their careers.

One of the most common learning disabilities, dyslexia, interferes with a person's ability to read. People with dyslexia report that words and sentences are hard to decode. Because they worry about performance and their slower rate of reading, students with dyslexia often feel singled out in classes for "not trying" or "failing to live up to your potential" despite the fact that they try hard to keep up.

If you find that your grades don't match your level of understanding, seek an evaluation for a learning disability.

Evaluate Your Issues

Many students think they have learning disabilities when they really don't. Sometimes they simply don't put in enough study time or their anxiety sabotages them on tests. When you confer with your advisor about your academic struggles, prepare an honest evaluation of how much work you're putting in on your studies. Your problems may lie in ineffective study strategies rather than a learning disability.

If you've experienced criticisms about your performance even though you're trying hard, you may find it helpful to work with a counselor or academic support person who can test you for learning disabilities. Diagnostic testing will determine whether you should seek further support.

Know Your Rights

If you have a learning disability, your academic outlook can still be good. Students whose learning difference can be verified by a qualified examiner may apply for special education support through the Education for All Handicapped Children Act of 1975. In addition, the Americans with Disability Act encourages campuses to support the special needs of students with disabilities. Many instructors have developed their own strategies to assist students. For example, they may offer longer test periods for students with language processing problems.

Compensate

If you do have a learning disability, you'll need to develop a set of strategies to compensate for the challenges your learning style presents. Among other things, you can:

- Set up a study group to discuss course material with others.
- Compare your notes with a friend's after each class to see if you've missed any important details.
- Use audio versions of textbooks when available.
- Use a spell-checker.
- Get support from the campus study skills center.
- Ask friends to proofread your written work.
- Alert your instructors to your special needs.

The compensating strategies that you develop in college will continue to serve you throughout life.

Applying the Six Strategies for Success

How does the material in this chapter make you think about ways you can succeed in college, particularly in the area of study skills? Write down your personal insights from reading the chapter that help you make meaningful links to the six strategies for success described on page 61.

Putting It All Together

1. List a few important issues to consider when deciding where to study, when to study, and what to study.

2. What is the difference between lower-order and higher-order cognitive skills? Provide a few examples of each.

3. How do the different disciplines encourage different kinds of study? List some specific strategies for success in the discipline area you are considering for your major.

4. List three pros and three cons of working in study groups. Now write down a strategy for addressing each con.

5. How can learning disabilities influence study success? What can be done to address such disabilities?

6. Describe the difference between short-term memory and long-term memory. How can you use this information to improve your study strategies in the future?

7. Identify a place where you have a hard time studying, such as a bus, a noisy dorm room, or a crowded kitchen table. In your journal or on paper to turn in, write out three strategies that would help you make this place better for studying. Now try each one. Did they work? Why or why not? What did this teach you about your ideal study location?

8 > Succeed on Tests

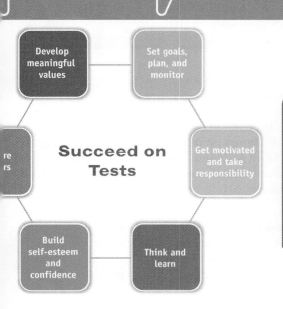

Develop meaningful values

Set goals, plan, and monitor

Get motivated and take responsibility

Succeed on Tests

re rs

Build self-esteem and confidence

Think and learn

As you read, think about the "Six Strategies for Success" listed to the left and how this chapter can help you maximize success in these important areas. For example, preparing for tests may be one of your strongest motivations to learn. Test taking can sharpen your planning skills, and your test results can clarify your career direction.

Plan for the Test

Successful test taking requires being organized and planning ahead. Using proven strategies in all of your courses will help you alleviate anxiety and be at your best.

Plan Ahead

You can apply these long-term strategies to maximize your success on all of your exams.

Pace Yourself Don't count on cramming! Eleventh-hour learning is fragile. It may crumble under pressure.

Meet Your Social Need If you have an extraverted style, studying with others will motivate you to do your reading and help to identify trouble spots. Ask other students who seem to understand the course—at least as well as you do, if not better—to join a study group. By contrast, if the stimulation of a study group is not compatible with your introverted style, find less socially intense support strategies.

Protect Your Health If you stay healthy throughout the term, you'll have fewer problems in managing your study schedule and fewer distractions at test time. You can't do your best if you're fighting off the urge to nap, feeling bad from a hangover, or coming down with a cold.

Adopt the Right Attitude Don't let test anxiety, a bad attitude, or poor planning get in the way of your success. Facing the test with the confidence that comes from conscientious planning and systematic study is the best way to overcome unproductive attitudes and emotions.

Prepare for the Test

Know What to Expect Test conditions vary. Your instructor may not even be present, so you might want to get all of your questions answered before the day of the test. In smaller classes with the instructor present, you may be able to clarify issues as they arise. Either during the class or in the syllabus, most instructors describe the kinds of tests they are planning. Some instructors even make sample tests from prior semesters available for study purposes. Many welcome questions about how to prepare. You may know some students who have completed the course before you. Find out what they did to succeed or what strategies didn't work.

"Psych out" the Teacher Some students seem psychic when guessing what will be on a test. How do they do it? They look for cues from the instructor that identify important and *testable* material (Appleby, 1997). Teachers may be signaling test material when they repeat certain concepts, illustrate key ideas with examples, intensify eye contact, use dramatic gestures, change their tone of voice, pause, write on the board or use a slide, or say "in summary" or "in conclusion."

Design Your Study Strategy Plan a suitable study strategy based on your learning style. Many tests, especially in introductory-level courses, focus on memorization. Your most effective memorization strategy will use your preferred sensory mode effectively. For example:

- *Visual learners* should use visualization techniques or drawings and diagrams to memorize material.
- *Auditory learners* may prefer to rehearse key ideas aloud or make up songs or rhymes to fix facts in memory.
- *Tactile learners* may try role-play or other hands-on strategies to add cues that help them recall information.

Other types of tests may focus on more sophisticated kinds of thinking. Find out what the format of the test will be ahead of time. Know how points will be distributed across the test. This knowledge may help you decide where to spend your time if it's clear you won't be able to finish. For example, the multiple-choice section may be worth 20 points, and the essay section 50 points. Even though the multiple-choice comes first, you may want to start with the essay, which counts for more. Find out whether there are penalties for guessing.

Succeed on Many Types of Tests

Objective Tests Memorizing facts is usually a good strategy for answering simple objective test questions. These include tests with multiple-choice, matching, true-false, and fill-in-the-blank items. Successful memorizing strategies include using flash cards, making a concept vocabulary list, reviewing a text's study guide, and reorganizing your notes. Find the memorizing strategy that works best for your learning style.

At the college level, most instructors ask objective questions that require more than just rote memory. When you have to do more than recall facts, your study strategy will also be more complex. Draw organizational charts or diagrams to identify relationships. Design some practice questions that exercise your ability to reason.

Essay Tests Digesting a whole term's worth of material for an essay can be a challenge. If you know the specific topics ahead of time, scan the notes you've made and highlight all related ideas in a specific color. This will let you concentrate on those ideas as you think about questions or practice answers. If you don't know the essay topics ahead of time, go back over your course and reading notes and write a paragraph for each text chapter or course lecture. These paragraphs would summarize the key ideas in the passage.

Procedural Tests Some types of tests ask you to demonstrate specific procedures, such as applying a formula to solve a math problem, conducting an interview in nursing, or solving for an unknown in chemistry. To prepare for procedural tests, perform the target skill until you're comfortable with it. If test time will be limited, build time limits into your practice.

Be Ready for the Test

It's almost here. Whether you're filled with dread or eager to show what you know, the following last-minute strategies give you the best chance of doing well.

- Get at least eight hours of sleep before the test.
- Bring a bottle of water or cup of coffee to keep up your spirits.
- Organize and bring required supplies and spares.
- Bring a dictionary, if permitted.

Overcome Test Anxiety

Just moments before your instructor hands out an exam, you may feel as if you're in the first car of a roller coaster about to hurtle down the first drop. Your heart pounds. You're sweating. The butterflies just won't go away. A few butterflies are okay. A little anxiety even can be a good sign. It encourages you to prepare for the test and can motivate you to do your very best.

Too many butterflies, though, can cripple your test performance. Nervousness and worry activate the emergency systems in your body. Your pulse increases. Your heart beats faster. Your hands perspire. These responses prepare you to flee or to fight. In stressful circumstances, they help you survive. But in the quiet of the classroom, they interfere with your ability to focus on the test.

Don't Sabotage Success

Test-anxious students sabotage their own efforts because they focus on themselves in negative ways (Kaplan & Saccuzzo, 1993). Preoccupied with the certainty of their own failure, they can't free up the energy to perform well. This reaction increases their chances of failure. Text-anxious students interpret even neutral events as further proof of their own inadequacy. For example, if a test proctor looks troubled, the test-anxious student may assume that her or his own behavior somehow caused the troubled look. Test-anxious students are more likely to experience stress-related physical symptoms, such as an upset stomach or a stiff neck, that further hinder performance. If you have anxiety about tests, you need to do two things:

1. Cope with your anxiety.
2. Improve study skills to build your competence and confidence (Zeidner, 1995).

If you learn to cope with anxiety but don't improve your study skills, you'll feel calmer and more in control but won't improve your performance. By contrast, if you improve your study skills but don't master your anxious feelings, your performance may still erode. It will take some effort to do both things, but consider the long-term rewards.

Master Anxiety

What are some specific things you can do to master test anxiety?

- *Invest your time properly.* Think about it. If you haven't spent as much time preparing for a test as you should, it makes sense to be frightened about performing poorly. Test jitters may only mean that you need to invest more time. If the format your professor will be using doesn't play to your strengths as a test-taker, allocate more time to compensate for this challenge.

- *Neutralize anxiety.* One simple strategy is to neutralize your anxious feelings by learning to breathe in a relaxed manner under stress.

- *Talk positively to yourself.* Test-anxious students often make their anxieties worse by predicting their own failure. Instead of tormenting yourself with criticism and dire predictions, substitute positive statements, such as "I will overcome this

making connections

If You Must, Cram Strategically

It's a bad idea to depend on cramming, but sometimes it can't be helped. You may have too many courses to manage any other way. What are some of the best ideas for last-minute, concentrated study?

Clear the decks
Dedicate your last study session before the test to only that exam. Studying anything else can interfere with the test at hand.

Use textbook study aids
The chapter headings and chapter end-matter can help you organize your last-minute study strategies by identifying key ideas before you begin reading. First, go through the book and look at the headings—in a good textbook, these will provide you with an outline of the key ideas in the chapter. This practice is especially appropriate in an introductory book. Then read the summary, and look at the key terms and review questions. You will get a pretty good idea of the most important material in the chapter.

Skim for main ideas
Once you know what to look for, skim the chapter with the key ideas in mind. You may even want to skim just to answer the review questions. Scan each paragraph in relevant readings for the key ideas. Topic sentences that capture the central idea of each paragraph are usually the first or the last sentences in the paragraph. Skim the entire assignment to improve your chances of remembering the material.

Divide and conquer
Once you've skimmed the entire body of study materials, size up how much you have to learn in relation to your remaining time. Divide the information into reasonable sections and make your best guess about which will have the largest payoff. Master each section based on whatever time you have left. Even if you don't get to the lower-priority material, your test performance may not suffer much.

Stay focused and alert
Study in good light away from the lure of your bed. Take regular breaks and exercise mildly to stay alert through your session. Caffeine in moderation and regular snacks also may help.

Be cautious about professional summaries
Use professional summaries of great works if you can't complete a full reading. If you rent a film version of a great work of literature, be aware that films and even professional summaries often depart from the original in ways that may reveal your shortcut.

Learn from your mistakes
When you enter a test feeling underprepared, you've undermined your ability to succeed. Even if you luck out and do well, this strategy shortchanges what you think and learn over the long term. Consider the factors that left you in such desperate study circumstances. Commit yourself to doing all you can to avoid getting stuck in a situation where you have to cram.

challenge" or "I feel confident I will do well." Practice an optimistic outlook and more positive self-esteem will follow.

- *Exercise regularly.* Many students find relief from their anxieties by building a regular exercise program into their busy schedules. Exercise is a great stress reliever. It also promotes deeper, more restful sleep.

- *Avoid drugs.* Monitor your caffeine intake. Too much can compound agitated feelings. But caffeine presents minor concerns compared with the problems that result from using more potent drugs to ward off anxiety or to stay alert.

Good study skills and relaxation techniques counter test anxiety.

Master Test-Taking Strategies

The following general strategies will help make the most of your studying to succeed on tests.

- *Relax.* Take a deep breath. The calmer you stay during a test, the better you'll do. Take relaxing breaths at the start and continue breathing calmly throughout the test.

- *Look at the entire test.* Examine the structure. Count the pages. Plan how to divide your time, given your strengths and weaknesses. If the test includes different types of questions (such as multiple-choice and short-essay), begin with the type you do best on to build your confidence. Leave more time for parts that require more effort or that make up more of your total score. Plan some time at the end to review your work.

- *Read the instructions. . .twice!* You'll be very upset if you discover near the end of the exam time that you were supposed to answer only certain questions rather than all the questions on the test. Read the instructions carefully. Then read them again.

- *When you get stuck, identify the problem and move on.* You'll be taking most exams under time pressure, so you can't afford to spend too much time probing the depths of your memory.

- *Concentrate despite distractions.* If you start daydreaming, circle the item that got you off task and come back to it later. Avoid getting caught up in competition with students who complete the test early. Do the test at your pace—don't worry about who gets done first.

- *Ask for clarification.* When you're confused, ask your instructor or proctor for help. Most instructors try to clarify a question if they can without giving away the answer. An instructor may even decide that the question doesn't work and will throw it out.

- *Learn from the test.* The test itself may jog your memory. One area of the test may hold clues that can help you with other areas.

- *Proofread your work.* Whether it's a series of math problems or an extended discussion on Japanese haiku, review your work. Under pressure, it's easy to misspell, miscalculate, and make other errors even on things you know well. Using clear editing marks on your test paper demonstrates that you were being as careful as possible about your work.

Master Multiple-Choice Strategies

You'll probably face many tests that are mainly multiple choice: "question stems" or incomplete statements, followed by possible answers from which to choose. The following strategies will help improve your scoring on multiple-choice questions.

- *Read the test items carefully and completely.* Read *all* the alternatives before you identify the best one. This is especially important when your instructor includes "All of the above" or "A and C only" types of choices.

- *Strike out wrong answers.* When you can't easily identify the correct answer, eliminate the wrong choices so you can concentrate only on real contenders.

- *Mark answers clearly and consistently.* Use the same method of marking your choices throughout the test. This may be important if questions arise later about an unclear mark. If your test is machine scored, avoid making extra marks on the answer sheet. They can be costly.

- *Change your answers cautiously.* Make sure you have a good reason before you change an answer. For example, change your answer if you mismarked your exam, initially misread the question, or clearly know you're moving to the correct alternative. If you aren't certain, it's best not to change. Your first impulse may be best.

- *Guess!!* Some tests subtract points for incorrect answers. In this case, answer only the questions that you know for certain. However, most multiple-choice tests give credit for correct answers without extra penalty for wrong answers. In this situation, guess. If the question has four alternatives, you have a 25 percent chance of being correct.

- *Look for structural clues.* If a choice does not work grammatically with the stem, it's probably not the right choice. In complex questions, the longest alternative may be the best one. The instructor may simply require more words to express a complex answer.

Master True-False Strategies

True-false questions ask you to make judgments about whether propositions about the course content are valid or truthful. For example, consider this item: "True or False: It is always a bad idea to change your answer." This would be a good true-false question to assess your understanding of the last section on multiple-choice questions. (The answer is "False.") To maximize your performance on true-false items:

- *Go with your hunch.* When you don't know the answer on a true-false question, you have a 50 percent chance of being right when you guess. Choose the alternative with the intuitive edge.

- *Don't look for answer patterns.* Instructors generally strive to make the order of true-false answers random.

- *Honor exceptions to the rule.* If you can think of exceptions to the statement, even one exception, then the statement is probably false. In the earlier example, if you can think of even one circumstance in which changing your answer is a good idea, then the statement should be marked "False."

- *Analyze qualifying terms.* Words that specify conditions, such as *always, usually,* and *never,* usually identify an item that is false. Those terms suggest an unlikely or unwarranted generalization. Notice in our example, "It is always a bad idea to change your answer," the word *always* makes the statement invalid, because there are some times when changing your answer makes sense.

Master Fill-in-the-Blank Strategies

Like multiple-choice questions, fill-in-the-blank questions test how well you recall information. An example of a fill-in-the-blank format is "Instructors try hard to make a _____ pattern of answers on true-false tests." (The answer is "random.") You probably either know or don't know the answers to these kinds of questions but you may recover some answers that you don't know initially by skipping them and returning to them after you complete the rest of the test. This process may cue you to come up with just the right fill-in.

Master Short-Answer Strategies

Short-answer questions demonstrate how well you can explain concepts briefly. For example, a short-answer question might be "Describe some strategies for doing well on true-false questions." To maximize your score on short-answer questions, write clear, logical, and brief answers. Writing a great deal more than asked, or including information not asked for, suggests that you do not understand the concepts. When you skip a short-essay question because it stumps you, look for cues in the rest of the test that may help you go back and answer it later.

Master Essay-Question Strategies

Essay questions evaluate the scope of your knowledge and your ability to think and write. They tend to be much more demanding than objective test questions. What are some steps you can take to do your best on essays?

- *Anticipate possible questions.* If you were in your teacher's shoes, what questions would you ask? For example, an essay question that you could predict about the material in this section could be "Compare and contrast multiple-choice and essay-question strategies as a way of measuring your learning."

- *Read the question carefully.* A well-developed answer won't help you capture points if you don't answer the right question.

- *Highlight the requested action.* For example, in our earlier sample question you could underline *compare and contrast* to keep you focused on the most successful approach.

- *Outline the key ideas.* A systematic blueprint can help you capture the most important ideas in your answer.

- *Represent the question in your opening sentence.* Don't waste time rewriting the question. Set the stage for the information that will follow, such as: "Instructors use multiple-choice and essay questions to evaluate how much you have learned from a course. These strategies share some similarities, but each offers some strategic advantages over the other."

- *Develop the main body of the essay.* Each paragraph should address an element required in the question: "The common characteristics of multiple-choice and essay questions include. . .Multiple-choice and essay questions also differ in what information they impart about a student's learning. . ."

- *Summarize only if you have time.* Write like a reporter—present key ideas first and follow with details. This practice increases the likelihood that you'll cover the most important and point-scoring information before you run out of time.

- *Write legibly.* If your handwriting gets worse under stress—slow down. Instructors can't give credit for what they can't decipher.

- *Proofread your work.* Under time pressure, your written language can easily escape your control. Go back over your work and make any corrections the instructor will need in order to understand you clearly. Don't worry about the mess. Your own editing marks show that you care about the quality of your thinking.

- *Don't bluff.* The longer you write and the more you ramble, the more you expose what you really don't know.

- *Use humor carefully.* Unless you have clear cues from your instructors that they would appreciate a lighthearted response, don't substitute humor for an effective answer.

Review Your Results

At some point in your college career, you may not perform as well on a test as you hoped you would. Sometimes instructors don't design tests effectively. At other times, you simply may be pushed in too many directions to concentrate and do your best. Or the course may be a bad match to your natural skills and interests.

Don't let yourself become undone by one failure. Frame this disappointment as an opportunity to do some good critical thinking to figure out the causes of your poor performance and to craft some new strategies to improve your situation. Begin this approach with a careful review of your test results.

Review Your Work

Some reviewing of your test results will help you do better on the next test. Review to:

- **consolidate** your learning,
- **analyze** what worked and what didn't work in your study strategy, and
- **ensure** that the grade was accurate.

Review all items, not just ones on which you made mistakes. Review and rehearse one more time the material that your instructor thinks you need to learn in the course. This can help you in the long run, especially if you have a cumulative exam at the end of the term.

Your test review should tell you whether your study strategy worked. Did you spend enough time studying for the test? Did you practice the right kinds of thinking to match the particular demands of this teacher? How can you use your study time more efficiently for the next test? Talk with the instructor about better ways to prepare.

What if your instructor doesn't allow extensive time for review of your exam during class—or worse, doesn't return the exams at all but only posts the grades? Visit your instructor during office hours and ask for the opportunity to review your test results. This visit also allows you to clarify any questions you have about your instructor's testing or grading practices, and shows that you are taking personal responsibility for your learning.

Check the grading. Instructors can easily make errors when applying test keys or counting up point totals. Also identify questions that were not clearly written. Even if your critique of a question does not persuade an instructor to change your grade, your review may give you insight into how the instructor constructs tests, which can help you on the next one. Instructors are unlikely to change a grade without good reason. Most construct tests carefully and grade them as fairly as possible. However, if you believe the instructor misunderstood you or made an error in calculating your score that affects your grade, by all means ask for a grade change. Remember, though, that instructors can't give you extra points if it gives you an unfair advantage over others in the class.

Applying the Six Strategies for Success

How does the material in this chapter make you think about ways you can succeed in college, particularly in terms of taking exams and tests? Write down your personal insights from reading the chapter that help you make meaningful links to the six strategies for success described on page 71.

Putting It All Together

1. How does a positive attitude influence your success on tests? List three strategies you can implement to improve your test performance in the future.

2. How should your study strategies vary according to the kind of test you'll be facing? List a few specific types of tests followed by a description of an appropriate study strategy.

3. Describe a few specific ways to overcome test anxiety.

4. Why should you review your test results carefully when the instructor returns your work? What else should you do after a test to maximize your overall grade in the course?

5. Rank the following test formats in the order of your preference: Fill-in-the-blank, multiple-choice, true-false, short-answer, and essay. In your journal or on paper to turn in, speculate about why you ordered the formats as you did. How does your achievement history influence your choice? Does your learning style dictate which formats are more appealing?

9 > Express Yourself

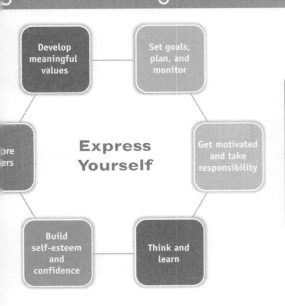

Develop meaningful values

Set goals, plan, and monitor

Get motivated and take responsibility

Express Yourself

Build self-esteem and confidence

Think and learn

As you read, think about the "Six Strategies for Success" listed to the left and how this chapter can help you maximize success in these important areas. For example, motivate yourself to practice your communication skills whenever you can. Setting and achieving communication goals will help you succeed in college and prepare you for any career.

Get Organized

Whether your project involves writing or speaking, the following strategies can help you produce your best effort.

Clarify Your Goal

Make sure you understand the goal of the assignment from the instructor's point of view. Look at the syllabus and try to link the specific assignment to the overall goals of the course. Ask questions to clarify anything that is unclear. Compare your ideas with your classmates' perceptions. Actively evaluate how the goal of the assignment can help you achieve your writing goals. For example, if your assignment is to write a three- to five-page essay, you might opt for the shorter three-page goal to help you work on developing short, coherent arguments. By contrast, if you receive feedback that you need to develop your ideas in greater depth, go for the five-page limit.

Define Your Purpose

Before you begin writing, review the directions and make sure you understand the purpose of the assignment. There are basically five reasons for writing:

- *To explain an idea or provide information (expository).* Research papers and essays often have this purpose. Instructors often assign research papers so that you can develop your research skills as well as your writing skills. Essays develop your writing and reasoning skills, and demonstrate your ability to think analytically about the subject you're learning.

- *To persuade or argue a point.* This type of assignment often combines writing and problem-solving skills. In a persuasive or argumentative writing assignment, you follow these steps: define the problem and its impact; describe the origin of the problem; identify other relevant factors; propose a solution; predict all of the outcomes of the solution; and develop a follow-up strategy.

- *To describe an experiment or process or to report on lab results.* In science classes, you may work independently or collaborate on a lab report that describes a specific scientific procedure. Lab reports are usually highly structured, based on a set of conventional headings. Usually a lab report includes an introduction, methods, results, and discussion.

- *To reflect on your own experience.* Journal writing lets you explore the personal significance of what you are studying. Although research may not be required in such projects, it's a good idea to connect your journal entries with course concepts to show what you have learned.

- *To create an original piece of writing.* Literature instructors may assign creative writing projects, such as poetry and short stories, to foster an appreciation of these genres. Don't rule out doing research for reflective assignments. Locate authors whose style you admire. Do some background reading on a topic that might focus your work.

Select a Topic

Many instructors will select your topic, at least in a general way. However, you still may have to narrow it down. Choosing well can help you take responsibility and embrace the work that lies ahead. What strategies can help?

1. Look through your notes. What concepts stand out as the most interesting to you?

2. Examine your textbook and course readings, explore the encyclopedia, or cruise the Internet to spark your imagination.

3. Explore your personal experience. Think about aspects of the assignment that naturally connect to your own life.

4. Consider what topic would be the most fun or would have the most future value for you. Are there topics that will connect in a meaningful way to your future career plans? Give those ideas top consideration.

Narrow Your Topic

As you explore possible topics, avoid ones that are too large, too obscure, too emotional, or too complicated for you to work with in the allotted time. Do not write or speak about areas where you have little knowledge because it's easier to stay engaged with a project in which you have personal interest. Conduct research until you have the knowledge you need to succeed. You may need to redefine the project several times before settling on a topic that speaks to you. Although a number of techniques exist for narrowing your topic once you have a general idea of what you want to write about, most approaches encourage you to "mess around" with the ideas to begin to make them your own (McKowen, 1996). Do some freewriting. Write without stopping for a while just to get some thoughts on paper. Or try brainstorming, in which you write down all of the concepts or ideas that occur to you on the topic. Talk to a friend to stir up ideas. Or try asking these questions about the topic: *who, what, when, where, why,* and *how?* Finally, do some reading on the topic to start the focusing process.

Develop a Working Thesis

After you have narrowed your topic to an area of specific interest to you, refine it even further by developing a *thesis*. Your *thesis statement* conveys your general position on the topic and guides the direction of your writing, which supports your thesis. The thesis is essential because it focuses your topic and provides a clear direction for your thinking, research, and writing.

A good working thesis:

1. Reduces the topic to a single controlling idea, unifying opinion, or key message

2. Presents your position clearly and concisely, in one sentence

3. Makes a statement that can be supported by statistics, examples, quotes, and references to other sources within the time and space constraints of the assignment

4. Creates interest in the topic

5. Establishes the purpose of the paper

6. Establishes the approach or pattern of organization

Don't be afraid to modify your thesis. If your research is not supporting it, restate your thesis to reflect the supporting evidence. Sometimes you will need to do some preliminary research before you can even write your thesis statement.

Write with Impact

Create Your First Draft

The draft stage is an important first step. However, don't confuse a first draft with a final presentation. Following are some important things to keep in mind when first drafting your assignment.

Know Your Audience Strike the right tone for your audience. For example, some tasks require objective and precise presentation of the facts. In other projects you must be exploratory and imaginative. Knowing your audience can help you make the right decisions.

Keep It Casual, and Keep It Moving In your first draft, you should try not to get bogged down. Write quickly. If you've done your research, and have given yourself enough time to think about the project, you'll be surprised at how much you know without referring to your note cards. Much of what you write comes from thinking that is done without you even knowing it.

You don't have to write in a particular order. Develop the points first that you know best and end with those that require more thinking or references to research. Consider writing your introduction last, and your conclusion first. This way you will know where you're going and can keep in mind that all paragraphs must lead to that ending. Set subgoals for how much writing you want to accomplish in any given sitting. For example, it may help to draft the conclusion one day and key paragraphs on other days.

Organize Your Argument Formal papers usually have three parts: an introduction, a body, and a conclusion. The introduction, which contains the thesis statement, lays a foundation for the rest of the piece. It creates a context for understanding the entire paper.

The body of the paper should include your opinions and the evidence that supports your argument. Each paragraph in the body should introduce a separate idea, and support it with details such as quotes, examples, statistics, and references to other sources. Each paragraph should follow logically from the one before, and all paragraphs must relate to the thesis of the paper. The body should use a clear pattern of organization such as listing patterns, comparison patterns, sequencing patterns, cycle patterns, problem-solving patterns, cause/effect patterns, definition/example patterns, and topical/categorical patterns, as discussed earlier in the text.

In a long paper, your conclusion should summarize your argument or review your main points. Make sure that your conclusions fit with the thesis statement you established at the beginning. You can say more about its implications for action or further study. In a short essay, the conclusion may just refer to the thesis or introduction. The conclusion represents your last opportunity to win over your reader.

Revise and Revise Again

Always leave plenty of time for revision. It is the single most important part of the writing process. In fact, you should plan to spend at least 50 percent of your time on this part of the writing process. You may have four or five working drafts before you reach the final draft.

After you have finished the first draft, put it aside for a couple of days. Each draft should be separated by at least a day of time away from the paper. This away time gives your brain a chance to process the material at a subconscious level, and allows you to come back to it with a fresh perspective.

Before you begin your revision, read it aloud to yourself or someone else. How does it sound? Does it flow? Does it make sense? Is it too long or too short? You may find you need to do more research to expand on certain points that don't seem adequately supported. You should go through and put a check next to the passages that are fine and a question mark next to any that require work.

Writers can keep unfinished work to themselves, but that stereotype isn't necessarily accurate. Most writers benefit from reviews by others. When your draft is almost finished, get feedback from others who write well. Ask them to point out places where you're not clear or to identify points that need further development.

Beginning writers sometimes struggle with knowing how much to write. Typically, they write too little rather than too much. Check your writing to see that you explained your intentions to the reader. Provide good examples. Make sure that the parts connect to each other with good transition sentences. All writing elements should follow logically from your original thesis statement.

Edit

Editing involves stylistic changes as well as modifying sentence structure and correcting spelling, punctuation, and grammatical errors.

Write with an active voice, using action verbs. Be specific, using descriptive language that draws on the senses; uses specific, concrete nouns; and avoids too many adverbs and adjectives. "It was a beautiful warm summer day" pales in comparison to "I sauntered out into a brilliant May morning, smiling at the lilting song of the diminutive sparrow and the sweet smell of my neighbor's manicured lawn."

Effective writers are careful about following the rules or *conventions* (for example, grammar, punctuation, and spelling) of good writing. Use a writer's reference manual to check on points you aren't sure about. Specific *style manuals* such as those published by the American Psychological Association (APA) and Modern Language Association (MLA) will also help you adjust to different disciplinary conventions. Ask your instructor which style manual is best for your purpose.

Smudge-free, easy-to-read writing says a great deal about your high standards and professionalism. Most instructors expect you to use word processing to produce your paper. That way you can revise easily. Include a cover page with the title of the paper, your name, your instructor's name, the course, and the date, unless your instructor requires a different format. Be sure to number the pages.

Proofread the final draft. You may be so close to what you've created that you can't spot errors easily. A break can help. By returning to the paper later, you can feel more confident about catching the subtle errors that you might miss when you are tired.

Do Your Research

Many writing and speaking assignments require research to flesh out facts, figures, and background information about your topic. Good research involves gathering reliable information from a variety of resources such as books, journals, and Internet sites.

Gather Sources

How many research sources should you include in your paper? Sometimes instructors will specify a minimum number; sometimes they won't. You may not have a clear idea about what will work best until you have done some research. Think responsibly about how many sources you will actually need to develop the most effective argument, but plan to look at more materials than you ultimately will refer to in your work. Not every resource you read will be relevant in the end. Choose those that help you develop a sound argument. Quality of evidence, not quantity, will impress your instructor.

Good researchers find and carefully show appropriate, persuasive evidence. For example, you can include statistics in a political science essay because numerical evidence communicates information about voting trends. Citing statistical evidence, however, in an expressive essay about literary criticism in a humanities class probably won't work. The point of any formal expressive assignment is to demonstrate your knowledge of course-related ideas.

As you do your research, also find sources that argue *against* your assertions. This practice may surprise you. Anticipating criticisms that the reader might have, and defending against them in your writing, strengthens your overall argument.

Write down the complete reference for each source *as you go*. It's frustrating to assemble a reference list at the end of your work only to discover that you forgot to write down the year a book was published, an important page number, or an Internet address.

Master the Library

Get to know your library's resources so you can locate information quickly. Take a tour if you haven't already done so. If you have trouble locating what you need, ask! Most librarians enjoy helping students. Approach the librarians who appear friendliest or pursue those with the most specialized knowledge on your topic.

Library searches often start in the reference room, which usually houses both paper and electronic databases. From there you may be routed to other areas of the library where you can locate original or *primary* sources (for example, books and journal articles), *secondary* sources (for example, textbooks and other sources that review primary works), or popular press items. References to research or expert opinions that you use in your research are called *citations*.

Your research assignment may specify which types of sources you can use. Most instructors prefer original (primary) sources. They also are more impressed by journal articles that are "peer reviewed." This means that the article was critically analyzed and then approved by other experts in the field. Check with your instructor whether some sources are off-limits, such as popular magazines. Once you've collected several sources, discard the unhelpful ones. Read those with potential carefully, taking notes that will help you represent the author's ideas. It can be helpful to collect pertinent information on three-by-five note cards that you can easily reorganize during the writing process.

Use the Internet

Whether you use the library or the Internet, your search will begin with a key word or two that you'll enter into an appropriate database. Do key word searches on several search engines to see what the nature of the discussion might be on the topic you have in mind. For example, if your environmental science class requires a paper on effective recycling strategies, start with the word *recycling*. Using that key word may produce so many search-engine hits that you could be overwhelmed. Narrow your search to something more specific such as *newspaper recycling* to find more targeted information. If your search produces too few hits, broaden the concept until you find some resources that will help you.

Relying on the Internet, however, can be risky. Most instructors still favor library research that will help you locate printed publications and peer-reviewed sources. The information on the Internet isn't always reliable. Anyone can post anything, making it hard to sift out the gold. Don't assume that an Internet source will be acceptable. However, instructors may be willing to accept Internet citations that are:

1. written by a recognized authority in the field
2. supported by a reputable host group
3. peer reviewed

Good research is important for many types of writing and speaking assignments, providing the basic information you then craft into your final presentation. Gathering your research notes on three-by-five cards is a good strategy for both writing and speaking projects.

making connections — Writer's Block

Sometimes you have nothing to say. Don't panic. All writers face times when inspiration fails and words don't come easily. Interestingly, one good response is to write about your writer's block. Write about how it feels to be empty. Describe the nature of your blocks. You may gain insight into your resistance and find ideas that will get you moving. Another good step is asking for a conference with your instructor.

By talking about the assignment, your instructor can offer tips or hints that can unleash your creativity. Ask whether your instructor has any model student papers. By observing how others tackled related problems, you may be able to spark some ideas of your own.

You also can try a creativity-generating computer program that provides a systematic approach to helping you plumb your ideas. *IdeaFisher* and *Inspiration* are two popular programs. Explore some other options by visiting this Internet site: http://members.ozemail.com.au/~caveman/Creative/Software/swin dex.htm.

Speak Up

Although both speaking and writing provide an opportunity to express yourself, speaking differs from writing in significant ways. When you write, you can refine your work until it says exactly what you want. However, when you speak, even though you can practice to a fine point, the reality of live performance adds a whole new communication challenge.

making connections → Prevent Plagiarism

Following are some strategies to help you avoid being accused of plagiarism during your college career.

Paraphrase When You Do Research
As you take notes from various resources, translate the ideas of others into your own words. Compare what you have written with the original source to make sure that your paraphrase captures the spirit of the ideas written, not the actual words and phrases themselves.

Give Proper Credit
When you directly quote or refer to the ideas of another writer, provide source information in the format required by your instructor.

Make Your Own Observations Stand Out In Your Notes
Put your own ideas in the margin or print them so that they look physically different from the ideas you received from others.

Use Quotations Sparingly
Rely on the words of experts only when their writing is so elegant that your paraphrase will not do it justice. Using many or long quotations is a sign that you're uncomfortable expressing your own ideas.

Don't Help Others Plagiarize
Lending others your papers when you suspect the borrowers plan to submit something based closely on your work implicates you in plagiarism.

Guard Against Others Plagiarizing Your Work
If you use a community-based computer, do not store your work on the computer's hard drive. Others who use the computer can easily download your writing and submit it as their own without your knowledge or permission.

Write a Good Speech

All famous speeches were written before they were delivered and became memorable. Keep in mind that the skills involved in preparing good papers also apply to good speeches. For example, you will want to develop a thesis statement, research your topic, create an outline, and organize your points into an introduction, main body, and conclusion. What additional strategies can you apply?

Define Your Purpose Know your goal. Are you supposed to persuade? Inform? Entertain? Debate? Your purpose will determine how to use resources and to structure your speech so you can achieve success. It also will help you avoid running too short or too long. Submit a thesis statement, outline, or concept map to your instructor before your scheduled presentation time. Ask for comments to help you stay close to the goal of the assignment.

Engage Your Audience Identify your purpose early in your speech. Keep in mind what your audience knows already and what they need to know. Never omit your purpose, however, even if the audience already knows it.

Build Your Message An anonymous speech instructor once recommended the perfect structure for public presentations, "Tell 'em what you are going to tell 'em, tell 'em, then tell 'em what you told 'em." Although this approach might sound boring, repeating the key ideas of a speech really counts.

Deliver a Good Speech

If you have invested time wisely in getting your ideas together, a speech gives you the opportunity to shine. How can you get the most out of these opportunities?

Rehearse The time put into rehearsal often makes or breaks a speech. If you know your speech well enough, you should need your note cards only for cues about what you intend to say. Otherwise, you may be tempted to read what you've written, which disconnects you from the audience.

Look the Part Dress to meet the expectations of the audience. For example, some formal speeches may work better if you dress less casually. How you dress should not distract from your message. You will want the audience to pay attention to your message, not your fashion sense.

Start your speech with a personal experience or a joke. Introduce an interesting news item, quotation, or event that the audience will remember. Conclude your opening with a statement of your objective and a description of where you intend to go.

Polish Your Delivery Stand straight and breathe in a controlled manner. Speak clearly and confidently. Make gestures that are purposeful, directing attention to underscore what you are saying. Look your audience in the eye. And don't forget to smile or frown appropriately to express the emotion you feel about your topic. Minimize the number of pauses, "ums" and "ahs," or other interruptions that invite your audience to stop listening. Use proper grammar. Effective speakers also project their voices to reach people at the back of the room and put life in their voices to keep people's attention.

Use Media Effectively You can use stories, video clips, quotations, statistics, charts, and graphs—whatever plays a meaningful role in the development of your position. If you use an overhead projector, computer-generated images, or PowerPoint slides, practice with the equipment before the speech since its use can be tricky.

Finish Gracefully When you conclude your speech, return to your key themes. Summarize what you've covered and identify any actions the audience should take as a result of your speech. If you've given a long speech, repeat your objectives.

Learn from Your Speeches

All great speakers suffer an occasional bad performance. Recognize your potential to learn from experiences that don't go well. Commit yourself to better preparation, goal setting, and improved performances in the future. See if you can work out a second chance with your instructor. Sometimes your speech can be videotaped in the college media facilities so the instructor can review it at a convenient time. Whether this second chance improves your grade or not, your positive practice will help you turn in a performance in which you have greater pride.

Applying the Six Strategies for Success

How does the material in this chapter make you think about ways you can succeed in college, particularly in terms of your writing and speaking skills? Write down your personal insights from reading the chapter that help you make meaningful links to the six strategies for success described on page 81.

Putting It All Together

1. Why are communication skills important for life after graduation? List a few ways that good writing and speaking skills can improve your job performance.

2. Describe at least three things you might want to accomplish in writing and speaking assignments.

3. Why should students avoid plagiarism? List a few strategies for making sure this doesn't happen to you.

4. What are some typical problems faced in giving formal speeches and how can these be overcome?

5. Recall a time when you observed someone making a bad speech.

   - At what point did you recognize the speech would be unsatisfying?
   - Did the speaker make any attempts to correct the failing outcome during the speech?
   - How did you feel as you watched the speech flop?
   - What advice could you have offered the speaker to turn the speech around?
   - How should these observations influence your preparation for future speaking challenges?

6. Begin a collection of papers from your courses to establish your writing portfolio. Arrange them in chronological order in a file folder or binder. What trends are apparent in the feedback that you are receiving?

   - Is the positive feedback you are getting consistent with your own self-image as a writer?
   - Is the negative feedback you are getting a clue about where you should concentrate your efforts to improve?
   - Do you see a potential research stream that you can capitalize on in future writing projects?

10 Develop Diverse Relationships

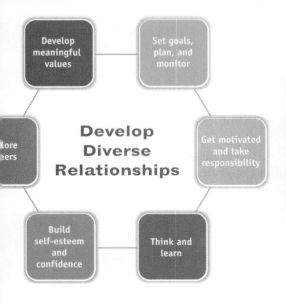

When employers are asked what they seek most in college graduates, the consistent answer is "communication skills." Thus, mastering communication skills will benefit you not only in college but in future careers and many other aspects of your life. So will building good relationships with many different kinds of people and appreciating their diversity. As you read, think about the "Six Points to Success" listed to the left and how this chapter can help you maximize success in these important areas.

Look, Listen, and Learn

In the back and forth exchanges of communication, messages can easily become garbled and misunderstood (DeVito, 2004; Tannen, 1986). Have you ever felt that someone was talking *to* you rather than *with* you? Or that a conversation was moving so fast that you couldn't keep up? Let's explore some ways you can become a better listener and speaker when you are communicating with someone.

Create Effective Verbal Communication

Messages are conveyed more effectively when you speak in a simple rather than a complex way, a concrete rather than an abstract way, and a specific rather than a general way. When you do need to convey ideas that are abstract, general, or complex, use appropriate examples to illustrate the ideas. Often the best examples are those that listeners can relate to their own personal experiences. For instance, if Margaret is trying to explain to some friends what feminism is and what it is like to be a feminist, it will help if she provides examples such as favoring equal opportunities regardless of gender, and then asks her friends to think about other people they know who are feminists.

Good speakers also make their verbal and nonverbal messages consistent. If you say one thing and nonverbally communicate the opposite, you are likely to create confusion and distrust. For example, if you are trying to explain to an instructor why you didn't turn a paper in on time and you look down at the floor rather than maintaining eye contact, the teacher may be less likely to believe you, even if your excuse is legitimate.

Good speakers also avoid barriers to effective communication. Consider Mike, who says, "I blew it again. When I went home last weekend, I vowed I wouldn't let my older brother get to me. We were only with each other for about ten minutes when he started in and I couldn't take his criticism any more. I started yelling and calling him names." Like Mike, we all too often want to communicate better with others but run into barriers we just can't seem to get around. Barriers to good communication include (Gordon, 1970):

- *Criticizing* (making negative evaluations): "It's your own fault—you should have studied."
- *Name-calling and labeling* (putting down the other person): "You're such an idiot for not planning better."
- *Advising* (talking down to the other person while giving a solution to a problem): "That's so easy to solve. Why don't you just . . . ?"
- *Ordering* (commanding the other person to do what you want): "Get off the phone, right now!"
- *Threatening* (trying to control the other person): "If you don't listen to me, I'm going to make your life miserable."
- *Moralizing* (preaching to the other person what he or she should do): "You know you shouldn't have gone there tonight. You ought to be sorry."

- *Diverting* (pushing the other person's problems aside): "You think *you* have it bad. Let me tell you about my midterms."
- *Logical arguing* (trying to convince the other person with logical facts without considering the person's feelings): "Look at the reasons why you failed. Here they are. . . . So, you have to admit I'm right." It's good to use logic to try to persuade someone, but if you lose sight of the person's feelings, no matter how right you are, the other person won't be persuaded and may be hurt.

Tune In to Nonverbal Communication

How do you behave when talking with others? Does the way you fold your arms, cast your eyes, move your mouth, cross your legs, or touch someone send a message?

Communications experts believe it does. You might:

- lift an eyebrow for disbelief
- clasp your arms to isolate or protect yourself
- shrug your shoulders for indifference
- wink one eye for intimacy
- tap your fingers for impatience
- slap your forehead for forgetfulness

These are conscious, deliberate gestures people make in the course of communicating. Are there also unconscious nonverbal behaviors that offer clues about what a person is feeling? Hard-to-control facial muscles especially tend to reveal emotions that people are trying to conceal. Lifting only the inner part of your eyebrow may reveal stress and worry. Eyebrows raised together may signal fear. Fidgeting may reveal anxiety or boredom.

Many communications experts believe that most interpersonal communication is nonverbal. Even if you're sitting in a corner silently reading a book, your nonverbal behavior communicates something—perhaps that you want to be left alone. It might also communicate that you're intellectually oriented.

You'll have a hard time trying to mask or control your nonverbal messages. True feelings usually express themselves, no matter how hard we try to conceal them, so it's good to recognize the power of nonverbal behavior (DeFleur and others, 2005).

What does the nonverbal communication in this photo reveal?

Manage Conflict

Use Assertiveness

Conflicts are inevitable in our everyday interactions, especially in an intense college environment. Developing skills to resolve these conflicts can make your life calmer and more enjoyable. Strategies for reducing interpersonal conflict include assertiveness and effective negotiation. Four main ways to deal with conflict are:

1. *Aggression.* People who respond aggressively to conflict run roughshod over others. They communicate in demanding, abrasive, and hostile ways often characterized by anger. Aggressive people often are insensitive to the rights and feelings of others.

Assertiveness builds equal relationships.

2. *Manipulation.* Manipulative people try to get what they want by making others feel sorry for them or feel guilty. They don't take responsibility for meeting their own needs. Instead, manipulative people play the role of the victim or martyr to get others to do things for them, working indirectly to get their needs met.

3. *Passivity.* Passive people act in nonassertive, submissive ways. They let others run roughshod over them. Passive people don't express their feelings or let others know what they want or need.

4. *Assertion.* Assertive people act in their own best interests. They stand up for their legitimate rights and express their views openly and directly. Assertiveness also builds equal relationships (Alberti & Emmons, 1995). Of the four styles of dealing with conflict, acting assertively is clearly the most appropriate. Assertiveness is an attitude as well as a way of acting. Be assertive in any situation in which you need to express your feelings, ask for what you want, or say "no" to something you don't want.

Negotiate Effectively

Everybody negotiates. You negotiate when you apply for a job, dispute a grade with a teacher, or buy a car. Whenever you want something from someone whose interests are at odds with your own, you can choose to negotiate.

Some negotiation strategies are better than others. Negotiating effectively helps you to get what you want from others without alienating them. Negotiation experts often describe three main ways of solving problems with others: win–lose, lose–lose, and win–win.

- *Win–lose strategy.* In this type of negotiating, one party gets what he or she wants and the other comes up short. In other words, "Either I get my way or you get your way." For example, a couple has a specific amount of money they can spend, but they totally disagree on how to spend it. Most of the time a win–lose

Take Charge of Your Anger

Everyone gets angry at one time or another. These strategies can help you take responsibility for controlling your anger (American Psychological Association, 2002; Tavris, 1989):

- When your anger starts to boil and your body is getting aroused, work on lowering your arousal by waiting. Your anger will usually simmer down if you just wait long enough.
- Slowly repeat a calm word or phrase, such as "relax" or "take it easy." Repeat it to yourself while breathing deeply.
- Change the way you think. Angry people tend to curse, swear, or speak in highly colorful terms that reflect their inner thoughts. When you are angry, you can exaggerate and become overly dramatic. Try replacing these thoughts with more rational ones. For example, instead of telling yourself, "Oh, it's awful, it's terrible, everything is ruined," say something to yourself like, "It's frustrating and it's understandable that I'm upset about it but it's not the end of the world and getting angry isn't going to fix it anyway."
- Don't say the first thing that comes into your head when you get angry. Rather, slow down and think carefully about what you want to communicate. At the same time, listen carefully to what the other person is saying and take your time before answering.
- Work on not being chronically angry over every little bothersome annoyance. Also, avoid passively sulking, which simply reinforces your reasons for being angry.
- Take the perspective of others and think about how you look to them when you get angry. Is this how you want others to think of you?

strategy is not wise. Why? Because the loser may harbor bad feelings and one person is always dissatisfied with the outcome.

- *Lose–lose strategy.* This usually unfolds when both parties initially try a win–lose strategy that does not work. As a result of the struggle, both end up unsatisfied with the outcome. In the money example, both individuals could end up spending too much and go deeply in debt.
- *Win–win strategy.* The goal in this strategy is to find a solution that satisfies both parties and to avoid winning at the other person's expense. By working together, they can find a solution that satisfies everyone. For example, after considerable discussion and negotiation, each member of the couple agrees to some concessions and they arrive at an agreeable spending plan.

Some compromises are often necessary in this win–win ideal. You and the seller settle on a price for a used car. The price is between what the seller was asking and what you wanted to pay. Neither of you got exactly what you wanted, but the outcome left each of you happy. Similarly, you and your companion each want to see a different movie. In order to spend the evening together, you might choose another movie that you both agree on.

The best solutions of all, though, are not compromises. Rather, they are solutions in which all parties get what they want. For example, Andrea and Carmen are roommates with different study habits. Andrea likes to study in the evening. This leaves most of her day free for other activities. Carmen thinks that evenings should be for relaxation and fun. They arrived at the following solution. On Monday through Wednesday, Andrea studies at her boyfriend's; Carmen does anything she wants. On Thursday and Sunday, Carmen agrees to keep things quiet where she and Andrea live. On Friday and Saturday they both have fun together.

The win–win strategy gives you a creative way of finding the best solution for a problem between two or more parties. You can use it to solve conflicts with others and make everyone involved feel better.

Develop Good Relationships

Relationships play a powerful role in college. As you think about your relationships, keep in mind that the strategies for communication, assertiveness, and negotiation we just discussed will serve you well.

Connect with Parents

No matter how much independence you want, it is not a good idea to break off communication with your parents. You'll likely need them at some point, possibly for money, a place to live, or emotional support. Keep in touch with them weekly, either by phone, letter, or e-mail.

If you're a young adult student in your first year, your parents may ask questions that seem intrusive. "How come you didn't get an A on your English test?" "Are you dating anyone?" "Have you been going to religious services?" Try to listen politely to their questions.

Be aware that your parents know only what you choose to tell them about your college experiences. According to the Federal Family Educational Rights and Privacy Act, the college cannot release your records to anyone but you. Instructors can discuss your progress or problems only in your presence or with your permission. This legal constraint encourages your family members to let you resolve your own problems. Use this control responsibly and wisely.

Relate to Spouse, Partner, and Children

Students who are married or have a partner face special challenges. Some strategies for keeping positive relationships with a partner include (Sternberg, 1988):

- *Don't take your relationship for granted.* Continue to nourish the relationship, giving it high priority along with your studies. Schedule time with your partner just as you do for classes and studying. Don't expect your partner to take over all of the household duties or to pamper you.

- *Develop self-esteem and confidence.* Don't seek in your partner what you lack in yourself. Feel good about your pursuit of education—it will enhance your confidence. When both partners have high self-esteem, their relationship benefits.

- *Share your college life.* Discuss your schedule, what you're learning, and what your day is like with your partner. Look for campus activities or events that you can attend together. To avoid being too self-focused, remember to ask about your partner's activities.

- *Be open with your partner.* While it may seem easier in the short run to lie or to hold back the painful truth, once omissions, distortions, and flat-out lies start, they tend to spread and ultimately can destroy a relationship. Talk becomes empty because the relationship has lost its depth and trust.

- *See things from your partner's point of view.* Ask yourself how your partner perceives you. This helps you to develop the empathy and understanding that fuel a satisfying, successful relationship.
- *Be a friend.* Researchers have found that one of the most important factors in a successful marriage is the extent to which the partners are good friends (Gottman & Silver, 1999). Friendship acts as a powerful shield against conflict.
- *Understand differences in communication style between men and women.* Men tend to view talk in a relationship as an opportunity to give information (Tannen, 1990). By contrast, women are more likely to view it as a way of exploring a relationship.

If you're a parent as well as a student, you also face special challenges. If your children are old enough, talk with them about how important they are to you as well as how important your education is. Each day set aside time to listen to your children.

At times, you may feel overwhelmed with juggling a family and school. Planning can be an important asset in your effort to balance your academic and family time. Check into child-care facilities and community agencies for services and activities for your children before and after school. However, be sure to block out at least some time each week for activities you enjoy or for relaxation.

Develop Responsible Dating Behavior

Dating can involve wonderful, happy times. It also can be a source of unhappiness, anxiety, and even violence. Some first-year students date frequently, others very little or not at all. Some students view dating as a way to find a spouse. Others see it as an important part of fitting into the social scene. Some students date for romantic reasons, others for friendship or companionship.

Too many first-year students get caught up in wanting to date an ideal rather than a real person. Some first-year students also look at every date as a potential girlfriend or boyfriend, someone they eventually might marry. College counselors say that such students would probably be better adjusted and happier if they broadened their perspectives. Don't look at every date as a potential Mr. or Mrs. Perfect. Dates can be potential friends as well as romantic partners.

Remember that forcing someone to engage in an unwanted act of sexual intercourse is rape. On campus, date or acquaintance rape is a particular problem. It is never acceptable to force or coerce sex from someone. At the same time, be sure to monitor your sexual feelings and engage only in sexual activities that you choose. Don't let fear, intoxication, or a sense of obligation get you into a situation you don't want to be in.

Appreciate Diversity

We should be accustomed to thinking of the United States as a country with many different cultures. Our population is diverse and originates from many different places, and college campuses are among the most diverse settings in this country.

Despite the opportunities to mix, people often associate with their "own kind." Think about where you eat lunch. Commuters often hang out with other commuters. Fraternity and sorority members sit off by themselves. Our fear of the unknown may keep us close to those whose background we share. This can prevent us from taking advantage of the rich opportunities on campus to meet and learn about people who differ from us.

According to a survey of students at 390 colleges and universities, ethnic conflict is common on many campuses (Hurtado, Dey, & Trevino, 1994). More than half of the African Americans and almost one fourth of the Asian Americans said that they felt excluded from college activities. Only 6 percent of Anglo Americans said that they felt excluded. Other research continues to show that a higher percentage of minority students experience discrimination (Biasco, Goodwin, & Vitale, 2001; Marcus & others, 2003).

Many of us sincerely think that we are not prejudiced. However, experts on prejudice believe that every person harbors some prejudices (Sears, Peplau, & Taylor, 2003). Why? Because we are naturally disposed to do it. We tend to identify with others who are like us. We tend to be *ethnocentric,* favoring the groups we belong to and tending to think of them as superior. We also tend to fear people who differ from us. All of these human inclinations contribute to prejudice, so we need to monitor ourselves in an effort to reduce such harmful attitudes.

Reduce Prejudice and Stereotyping

Think about these stereotypes: the blonde cheerleader; the computer nerd; the absent-minded professor; the Asian math whiz; the prim librarian; and the female basketball star. Notice that a simple label can conjure up an image and expectations about what a person will be like.

Now imagine that you get to know these people. You discover that:

- The blonde cheerleader has a 4.0 average.
- The computer nerd plays in a hot new jazz band at a local club on weekends.
- The absent-minded professor never misses a class.
- The Asian math whiz is only an average math student but is a campus leader who is very popular with her peers.
- The prim librarian gives freely of her time to local charities to help improve the lives of children.
- The female basketball star is dating a man in his second year of law school.

Clearly, stereotypes lead us to view others in limited and limiting ways. There's so much more to people than the social roles they play or the groups to which they belong (Jandt, 2004).

Prejudice is ugly and socially damaging and many people believe that college campuses should demonstrate leadership in reducing it. Recently, various diversity initiatives have been enacted to work toward this goal, including on-campus celebrations of ethnic achievements, festivals that highlight different traditions or beliefs, required coursework to explore traditions other than one's own, and inclusion of examples from a broader range of human experience in required readings. In spite of diversity initiatives, we still have a long way to go to reduce discrimination and prejudice.

Improve Your Relationships with Diverse Others

How can you get along better with people who differ from you? Here are some helpful strategies.

Assess Your Attitudes One of the first steps is to understand your own attitudes better. Are there people you don't like because of the group they belong to? Honestly evaluate your attitudes toward people who:

- are from different cultures
- are from different ethnic groups
- are of the opposite sex
- have a different sexual orientation

Take the Perspective of Others You can improve your attitude toward others by clarifying your perspective and trying to better understand that of others. Ask yourself what about that person's background, experience, and situation makes them different from you? In what ways are you similar?

Seek Personal Contact Martin Luther King, Jr., once said, "I have a dream that my four little children will one day live in a nation where they will not be judged by the color of their skin but by the content of their character." How can we reach the world King envisioned, a world beyond prejudice and discrimination? Mere contact with people from other ethnic groups won't do it. However, a particular type of contact—personal contact—often is effective in improving relations with others (Brislin, 1993). When we reveal information about ourselves, we are more likely to be perceived as individuals than as stereotyped members of a group. When we share personal information with people we used to regard as "them," we begin to see that they are more like "us" than we thought.

The more you get to know someone who seems different from you, the more similarities you will discover.

Respect Differences but Don't Overlook Similarities Think how boring our lives would be if we were all the same. Respecting others with different traditions, backgrounds, and abilities improves communication and cooperation. When we perceive people as different from us, we often do so on the basis of one or two limited characteristics such as skin color, sex, age, or a disability. When someone seems different, do you ever try to see how the two of you might be similar?

Search for More Knowledge In many instances, the more you know about people who are different from you, the better you can interact with them. Learn more about the customs, values, interests, and historical background of such people. Take a course on cultures around the world, for example.

Treat People as Individuals In our culture, we each want to be unique. You will get along much better with others who seem different if you keep in mind that they are individuals than if you think of them as members of a group. Talk with them about their concerns, interests, worries, hopes, and daily lives. Avoid stereotypes.

Applying the Six Strategies for Success

How does the material in this chapter make you think about ways you can succeed in college, particularly in terms of your relationships with family, friends, and acquaintances? Write down your personal insights from reading the chapter that help you make meaningful links to the six strategies for success described on page 91.

Putting It All Together

1. What are three basic strategies you can use to improve your communication skills? List at least one situation in which you can practice each strategy.

2. Describe a conflict you are currently experiencing or anticipate in the near future. What are some strategies you can apply to this problem?

3. List a few common problems you are having in your relationships with roommates or other individuals. What are some positive ways of addressing these issues?

4. Describe at least three strategies for combating loneliness. How can these strategies also help you build relationships and network on campus?

5. What types of diversity do you encounter on a regular basis? How can the strategies described in this chapter help you improve your relationships with diverse others?

6. What life experiences have you had with discrimination and prejudice? The discrimination might have been directed at you, or someone else. What were the consequences? If the discrimination took place in school, did anyone do anything about it? The discrimination doesn't have to be about race or gender. You might have been discriminated against because of the part of the country you're from, the way you dress, or how you style your hair. If you were discriminated against, how did you feel? If it was someone else, how did you respond? Write your responses in your journal or on paper to turn in.

11 > Be Healthy

Develop meaningful values

Set goals, plan, and monitor

ore ers

Be Healthy

Get motivated and take responsibility

Build self-esteem and confidence

Think and learn

As you read, think about the "Six Strategies for Success" listed to the left and how this chapter can help you maximize success in these important areas. For example, maintaining good physical and mental health gets you in shape to reach your academic goals. Your self-esteem is also closely linked to your health.

Value Your Health

How much do you value your physical and mental health? Like other achievements, strong physical and mental health is supported by setting goals, planning how to achieve them, and monitoring progress. Like everything worthwhile, your vigor and health depend on your values and motivation. Self-esteem also follows from physical and mental health, and vice versa. If you have high self-esteem you're more likely to embark on a program of improvement than if you have low self-esteem. If you're fit, you'll tend to have higher self-esteem. As you can see, your health is closely linked with many of the strategies for success already discussed.

Good health requires good health habits. By making some lifestyle changes, you may be able to live a much longer, healthier, happier life. In fact, as many as seven of the ten leading causes of death (such as heart disease, stroke, and cancer) can be reduced by lifestyle changes, yet most of us tend to deny that the changes we think *other* people need to make also apply to us. For example, in one study most college students said that they never would have a heart attack or a drinking problem but that other college students would (Weinstein, 1984).

Know the Risks to College Students

If you are like many college students, you're not nearly as healthy as you could be. In a recent national survey of first-year students, half said their health could be improved (Sax & others, 2001). Male college students engage in riskier health habits than females. For example, they are less likely to consult a physician or health care provider when they have unfamiliar physical symptoms, less likely to go to scheduled health checkups, and more likely to be substance abusers (Courtenay, McCreary, and Merighi, 2002).

Young adults have some hidden health risks. Ironically, one risk stems from the fact that they often bounce back quickly from physical stress and abuse. This can lead them to abuse their bodies and neglect their health. The negative effects of abusing one's body do not always show up immediately. However, at some point later one may pay a stiff price.

The following lifestyle patterns have been linked with poor health in college students: skipping breakfast or regular meals, relying on snacks as a main food source, overeating, smoking, abusing alcohol and drugs, avoiding exercise, and not getting enough sleep. Do any of these habits apply to you?

Are you relying on snacks or junk food to keep you going?

Do a Health and Lifestyle Check

Throughout this book, we have emphasized how important it is for you to take responsibility for your behavior. Your physical health is no exception. Exercising regularly, getting enough sleep, eating right, not smoking, avoiding drugs, and making the right sexual decisions all require you to consistently take charge of your life and not let yourself slide into bad habits.

Five steps in developing a self-control program to improve your health are (Pear & Martin, 2003):

1. Define the problem
What would you like to change? Which aspect of your health would you like to more effectively control? For one person, this might be "lose 30 pounds," for another it might be "quit smoking," and for yet another person it might be "engage in aerobic exercise for 30 minutes, four days a week." What aspect of your health do you want to change?

2. Commit to change
When college students commit to change, they become better self managers of their smoking, eating, exercise, and other aspects of their lives. Some good strategies for committing to change are:

- Tell others about your commitment to change—they will remind you of your commitment.
- Rearrange your environment to provide frequent reminders of your goal, making sure the reminders are associated with positive benefits of reaching your goal.
- Plan ahead for ways that you can deal with temptation, tailoring these plans to your program.

3. Collect data about yourself
This is especially important in decreasing excessive behaviors such as overeating and frequent smoking. Make up a chart and monitor what you do everyday in regard to what you want to change.

4. Design a self-control program
A good self-control program usually includes both long-term and short-term goals and a plan for how to reach those goals.

5. Make the program last
Establish specific dates for postchecks. Establish a buddy system by finding a friend with a similar problem. The two of you can set maintenance goals and check each other's progress once a month.

Address Health Problems

You should seek medical attention without delay if you experience any of the following (Vickery & Fries, 2000):

- a lump in your breast
- unexplained weight loss
- a fever for more than a week
- coughed-up blood
- persistent or severe headaches
- fainting spells
- unexplained shortness of breath

In some circumstances, these symptoms can signal a cancer or other serious problems. In many cases, though, a thorough medical exam will confirm that nothing serious is wrong. Either way, it is always best to be well informed about your health.

Keep a Healthy Body

Exercise Regularly

It's important to make good choices for a healthy body. Exercise is one important choice. In a national survey of first-year college students, regular exercise was linked with good health, and heavy TV viewing was related to poor health (Astin, 1993). In recent research, exercise has been shown to actually generate new brain cells.

Additional health benefits associated with exercise include improved cardiovascular fitness, greater lean body mass and less body fat, improved strength and muscular endurance, improved flexibility, greater life expectancy, fewer stress symptoms, improved mood and less depression, and higher self-esteem.

Clearly, exercise alone is not going to ensure that you reach your academic goals. However, the fact that it can help you generate new brain cells is linked with thinking and learning. What are some other ways the benefits listed above might help improve academic performance?

Get Some Sleep

In addition to getting adequate exercise, you should make sure you are getting enough sleep. Many college students deliberately pull all-nighters now and then to cram for a test. In a national survey, more than 80 percent of first-year college students said they stayed up all night at least once during the year (Sax & others, 1995). More common than all-nighters are successive nights with significantly reduced sleep because of parties, talking late with friends, and studying late. Just living with other students can produce irregular sleep patterns.

Take the responsibility of saying no to staying late at parties, or going out late when you have an early class. Unless it is an emergency, rather than staying up late when some friends just want to talk, set aside a time during the next day to talk with them. Many students think that sleeping late on the weekends makes up for lost sleep, but research recently has shown that this is not the case (Voelker, 2004). College students have twice as many sleep problems as the general population (Brown, Buboltz, & Soper, 2001). Caffeine, alcohol, and nicotine all interfere with sleep as well.

Most students need at least eight hours of sleep to function competently the next day (Maas, 1998). Researchers have found that many college students do not get this much sleep and, therefore, do not function at optimal levels the following day (Dement & Vaughan, 2000). In addition to academic problems, sleep deprivation is associated with higher levels of stress, headaches, inability to concentrate, less effective memory, irritability, and possibly increased susceptibility to illness (Insel & Roth, 2002).

Eat Right

Many college students have poor eating habits. A recent study of 1,800 college students found that 60 percent eat too much artery clogging saturated fat and 50 percent don't get enough fiber in their diet (Economos, 2001). Almost 60 percent said that they know their diet has gone downhill since they went to college.

- Get into a regular daily routine that lets you go to sleep and wake up at approximately the same time each day.
- Do something relaxing before you go to bed.
- Avoid discussing stressful problems before you go to bed.
- Make sure your sleeping area is good for sleeping.
- Cut out naps.
- Engage in regular exercise.
- Manage your time effectively.
- Manage your stress.
- Contact your college health center for professional help.

The "freshman 15" refers to the approximately 15 pounds that many first-year students gain. The weight often shows up in the hips, thighs, and midsection. Why do first-year students gain this weight? During high school many students' eating habits are monitored by their parents, so they eat more balanced meals. Once in college, students select their own diets, which often consist of chips, chips, and more chips, fast food, ice cream, late-night pizza, and beer. Once the extra 15 pounds arrive, what do first-year students do? They diet. Dieting is a way of life for many college students.

Be wary of diets that promise quick fixes or that sound too good to be true. Aim for a long-term plan that involves eating a variety of vegetables, fruits, and grains, and being physically active on a daily basis. This plan may produce slower results, but it works far better over the long term and is much healthier for you (Mayo Clinic, 2004).

One of the best sources of nutritional advice, the *Dietary Guidelines for Americans,* is issued jointly by the U.S. Department of Health and Human Services and the Department of Agriculture. These guidelines are revised every five years. The most recent ones support these three principles:

1. *Eat a variety of nutrient-dense foods.* Use the five basic food groups to evaluate your diet: milk and dairy, fruits, vegetables, grains, and meat and beans (which includes nuts and fish). Healthy adults need to eat at least three servings of vegetables, two of fruit, and six of grain products every day.

2. *Maintain a healthy weight.* Preoccupation with dieting can lead to dangerous loss/gain cycles that are hard on your body. Strive to maintain a reasonable, manageable weight.

3. *Follow a diet low in saturated and trans fats, and cholesterol.* Fat is found in large quantities in fried foods (fried chicken, doughnuts), rich foods (ice cream, pastries), greasy foods (spare ribs, bacon), and many spreads (butter, mayonnaise).

Anorexia Nervosa Most anorexics are white female adolescents or young adults from well-educated middle- and upper-income families. They have a distorted body image, perceiving themselves as overweight even when they become skeletal. Numerous causes of anorexia nervosa have been proposed (Smolak & Striegel-Moore, 2002). One is the current fashion image of thinness, reflected in the belief that a woman can never be "too rich or too thin." Many anorexics grow up in families with high demands for academic achievement. Unable to meet these high expectations and to control their grades, they turn to something they can control: their weight.

Bulimia *Bulimia* is a disorder that involves binging and purging. Bulimics go on an eating binge and then purge by vomiting or using a laxative. Sometimes the binges alternate with fasting. However, bulimics can also alternate with normal eating. Anorexics can control their eating; bulimics cannot. Depression is common in bulimics. If you have anorexic or bulimic characteristics, go to your college health center for help.

Limit Your Exposure to Risks

The best way to protect your health is to avoid unnecessary health risks, such as smoking, drug or alcohol abuse, and risky sexual behavior.

Don't Smoke

Some stark figures reveal why smoking is called suicide in slow motion:

- Smoking accounts for more than one fifth of all deaths in the United States.
- It causes 32 percent of coronary heart disease cases in the United States.
- It causes 30 percent of all cancer deaths in the United States.
- It causes 82 percent of all lung cancer deaths in the United States.
- Passive smoke causes as many as 8,000 lung cancer deaths a year in the United States.

Do you want to quit smoking? Many strategies and resources can help you quit. They include drug treatments, hypnosis, and behavior modification. Drug treatments include *nicotine gum* and *lozenges,* nonprescription drugs that smokers chew or suck on when they get the urge for a cigarette. Another drug treatment is the *nicotine patch,* a nonprescription adhesive pad that delivers nicotine through the skin. The dosage is gradually reduced over 8 to 12 weeks. Some smokers, usually light smokers, can quit cold turkey.

Avoid Drugs

Many college students take drugs (including alcohol) more than they did in high school. Some of the reasons why students increase their use of drugs in college are greater freedom from parental supervision, high levels of stress, and peer pressure to use drugs recreationally.

Drugs help people adapt to or escape from an ever-changing, stressful environment. Smoking, drinking, and taking drugs can reduce tension and frustration, relieve boredom and fatigue, and help us to ignore the world's harsh realities. Drugs can give us brief tranquility, joy, relaxation, kaleidoscopic perceptions, and surges of exhilaration. They sometimes have practical uses; for example, amphetamines can keep you awake all night to study for an exam. We also take drugs for social reasons. We hope they will make us feel more at ease and happier at parties, on dates, and in other anxious social contexts.

However, the use of drugs for personal pleasure and temporary adaptation can be dangerous. The use can lead to drug dependence, personal distress, and in some cases fatal diseases. What initially was intended for pleasure and adaptation can turn into pain and maladaptation.

Alcohol abuse is a special concern. Alcohol is the most widely used drug in our society. More than 13 million people in the United States call themselves alcoholics. Alcoholism is the third leading killer in the United States. Each year about 25,000 people are killed, and 1.5 million injured, by drunk drivers. More than 60 percent of homicides involve the use of alcohol by either the offender or the victim. About two thirds of aggressive sexual acts toward women involve the use of alcohol by the offender.

In a recent national survey, almost half of U.S. college students say they drink heavily (Wechsler & others, 2002). In this survey, almost 75 percent of underage students living in fraternities and sororities were binge drinkers (defined as men who drank five or more drinks in a row and women who drank four or more drinks in a row at least once in the two weeks prior to the survey) and 70 percent of traditional-age college students who lived away from home were binge drinkers. The lowest rate of binge drinking—25 percent—occurred for students living at home with their parents.

Almost half of the binge drinkers reported problems that included missed classes, injuries, troubles with police, and unprotected sex. Binge-drinking college students were eleven times more likely to fall behind in school, ten times more likely to drive after drinking, and twice as likely to have unprotected sex than were college students who did not binge drink. Date rape also is far more likely to occur when one or both individuals has been drinking heavily.

Do you have a substance abuse problem? What can you do about it?

- *Admit that you have a problem.* This is tough. Many students who have a substance abuse problem won't admit it. Admitting that you have a problem is the first major step in helping yourself.

- *Listen to what others are saying to you.* Chances are that your roommate, a friend, or someone you've dated has told you that you have a substance abuse problem. You probably denied it. They are trying to help you. Listen to them.

- *Seek help for your problem.* Among the numerous resources for students who have a substance abuse problem are Alcoholics Anonymous, Cocaine Anonymous, Al-Anon, and Rational Recovery Systems. Most towns have one or more of these organizations, which are confidential and are led by people who have successfully combatted their substance abuse problem. They can help you a great deal. Also, the health center at your college can provide help.

Make the Right Sexual Decisions

Making smart sexual decisions has never been more important than today. AIDS, other sexually transmitted diseases, and unwanted pregnancy pose life-altering challenges (Crooks & Bauer, 2004). Individuals vary in the extent to which they believe it is acceptable to engage in various sexual behaviors.

Avoid Sexually Transmitted Infections

Sexually transmitted infections (STIs) are diseases contracted primarily through sex. This includes intercourse as well as oral–genital and anal–genital sex. STIs affect about one of every six adults.

Common STIs include genital herpes, chlamydia, human papilloma virus (HPV), gonorrhea, hepatitis B, hepatitis C, and HIV/AIDS. With certain STIs, you may be showing no immediate symptoms and yet still pass the infection on to someone else who will suffer. Other STIs do cause symptoms, such as unusual discharge, burning during urination, painful bumps or sores, or warts.

No single STI has had a greater impact on sexual behavior or created more fear in the last decade than HIV/AIDS. Experts say that AIDS can be transmitted by sexual contact, sharing hypodermic needles, blood transfusion, or other direct contact of cuts or mucous membranes with blood or sexual fluids (Hyde & DeLamater, 2005). It's not who you are but what you do that puts you at risk for getting AIDS. *Anyone* who is sexually active or uses intravenous drugs is at risk. No one is immune.

Reduce Your Chances

What can you do to reduce the likelihood of contracting an STI? First, recognize that the only completely effective strategy is abstinence. But if you do choose to have sex, here are some ways to reduce your chances of being infected (Crooks & Bauer, 2005):

1. *Assess your and your partner's risk status.* If you've had previous sexual activity with others, you may have contracted an STI without knowing it. Have you been tested for STIs in general? Remember that many STIs don't produce detectable symptoms. Spend time getting to know a prospective sexual partner before you have sex with him or her. Ideally, this time frame is at least two to three months. Use this time to convey your STI status and inquire about your partner's. Keep in mind that many people are not honest about their sexual history.

2. *Obtain prior medical examinations.* Many experts on sexuality now recommend that couples who want to begin a sexual relationship abstain from sexual activity until both undergo medical and laboratory testing to rule out the presence of STIs. If cost is an issue, contact your campus health service or a public health clinic in your area.

3. *Use condoms.* When correctly used, condoms help to prevent the transmission of many STIs. Condoms are most effective in preventing chlamydia, gonorrhea, syphilis, and AIDS. They are less effective against the spread of genital herpes and genital warts.

4. *Avoid having sex with multiple partners.* One of the strongest predictors of getting AIDS, chlamydia, genital herpes, and other STIs is having sex with multiple partners.

Protect Against Unwanted Pregnancy

Most college students want to control whether and when they have children. That means either abstaining from sex or using effective contraception. Students who feel guilty and have negative attitudes about sexuality are less likely to use contraception than are students who have positive attitudes about sexuality.

You have many choices for contraception, including abstinence, oral contraceptives ("the pill"), condoms, a diaphragm, and spermicides. There are also long-term or permanent solutions such as the IUD, Norplant, Depo-Provera, tubal ligation, and vasectomy. Except for abstinence, no contraceptive is 100 percent effective. Know the failure rates and side effects of any contraceptive before you use it.

FIGURE 11.1 Effectiveness of Contraceptive Methods

The following are birth control methods and their failure rates in one year of average use.

Method	Unintended Pregnancy Rate* (percent)
No method (chance)	85.0
Spermicides	30.0
Withdrawal	24.0
Periodic abstinence	19.0
Cervical cap	18.0
Diaphragm	18.0
Condom	16.0
Pill	6.0
IUD	4.0
Tubal ligation	0.5
Depo-Provera	0.4
Vasectomy	0.2
Norplant	0.05

*Figures are based on women of reproductive age, 15 to 44. Rates vary with age. Failure rates with perfect use are lower, but people rarely use methods perfectly.
Source: *From Susan Harlap, et al.,* Preventing Pregnancy, Protecting Health: A New Look at Birth Control Choices in the United States, *Table 8.1, Alan Guttmacher Institute, New York and Washington, D.C., 1991.*

Stress is undoubtedly a factor in your mental health. However, do you know how important it is? According to the American Academy of Family Physicians, two thirds of all medical office visits are for stress-related symptoms. Stress is also a major contributor to heart disease, accidental injuries, and suicide.

Coping with stress is essential to making your life more productive and enjoyable (Blonna, 2005). Here are some techniques for coping (Folkman & Moskowitz, 2004).

See Stress as a Challenge Rather Than a Threat To cope successfully, it helps to (1) see the circumstances as a challenge to overcome rather than an overwhelming, threatening stress and (2) have good coping resources such as friends, family, a mentor, and the counseling center at your college (Lazarus, 1998).

Develop an Optimistic Outlook and Think Positively Thinking positively helps to put you in a good mood and improves your self-esteem. It also gives you the sense that you're controlling your environment rather than letting it control you. Thinking positively improves your ability to learn. A negative outlook increases your chances of getting angry, feeling guilty, and magnifying your mistakes.

Seek Emotional Support Knowing that others care about you can give you the confidence to tackle stressful circumstances.

Relax Many activities can be relaxing. You may also want to try *deep relaxation,* a technique that involves slowly entering a relaxed state through muscle tightening and release. Your counseling center can help you learn more about deep relaxation.

Write about Your Stress Writing about your stress not only provides a release of pent-up tension but also can stimulate you to think about ways to cope more effectively with the stress (Pennebaker, 2001).

Applying the Six Strategies for Success

How does the material in this chapter make you think about ways you can succeed in college, particularly in terms of your physical and mental health? Write down your personal insights from reading the chapter that help you make meaningful links to the six strategies for success described on page 101.

Putting It All Together

1. List three strategies you can implement to exercise, sleep, and eat better.

2. What are some effective strategies for kicking a smoking, drug, or alcohol habit? List a few ways drug use can negatively impact your success in college.

3. What can you do to protect yourself from sexually transmitted diseases and unwanted pregnancy?

4. Think of three effective methods you would use to cope with stress.

5. List your healthy eating habits and your unhealthy habits. Then think of ways you can replace unhealthy habits with healthy ones.

12 ⟩ Explore Careers

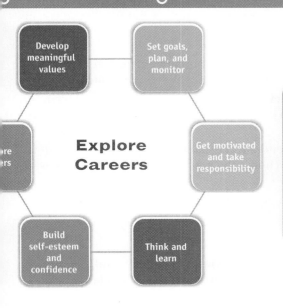

As you read, think about the "Six Strategies for Success" listed to the left and how this chapter can help you maximize success in these important areas. For example, linking your values with your career goals will help motivate you through college.

Assess Your Skills, Interests, and Options

Skills include both your academic and personal strengths. We develop some skills easily while others are more difficult to learn. Honestly evaluating your areas of strength and weakness will help you a great deal in realistically appraising majors and careers.

Assess Your SCANS Factors

The U.S. Department of Labor issues reports created by the Secretary's Commission on Achieving Necessary Skills (SCANS). The SCANS reports describe skills and personal qualities that will benefit individuals as they enter the workforce. It focuses on four types of skills and personal qualities (basic, thinking, personal, and people). Which skills represent areas of strength or weakness for you?

Basic Skills

- **Reading:** Identify basic facts, locate information in books and manuals, find meanings of unknown words, judge accuracy of reports, and use computers to find information
- **Writing:** Write ideas completely and accurately in letters and reports with proper grammar, spelling, and punctuation; and use computers to communicate information
- **Mathematics:** Use numbers, fractions, and percentages to solve problems; use tables, graphs, and charts; and use computers to enter, retrieve, change, and compute numerical information
- **Speaking:** Speak clearly and select language, tone of voice, and gestures appropriate to an audience
- **Listening:** Listen carefully to what a person says, noting tone of voice and body language, and respond in a way that indicates an understanding of what is said

Thinking Skills

- **Creative Thinking:** Use imagination freely, combining information in innovative ways and making connections between ideas that seem unrelated
- **Problem Solving:** Recognize problems, identify why a problem is a problem, create and implement solutions to problems, observe to see how effective a solution is, and revise as necessary
- **Decision Making:** Identify goals, generate alternatives and gather information about them, weigh pros and cons, choose the best alternative, and plan how to carry out your choice
- **Visualization:** Imagine building an object or system by studying a blueprint or drawing

Personal Qualities

- **Self-Esteem:** Understand how beliefs affect how a person feels and acts, listen and identify irrational or harmful beliefs that you may have, and know how to change these negative beliefs when they occur

- **Self-Management:** Assess your knowledge and skills accurately, set specific and realistic personal goals, and monitor progress toward goals
- **Responsibility:** Work hard to reach goals even if a task is unpleasant, do quality work, and have a high standard of attendance, honesty, energy, and optimism

People Skills

- **Social:** Show understanding, friendliness, and respect for others' feelings; be assertive when appropriate; and take an interest in what people say and why they think and behave the way they do
- **Negotiation:** Identify common goals among different people, clearly present your position, understand your group's position and the other group's position, examine possible options, and make reasonable compromises
- **Leadership:** Communicate thoughts and feelings to justify a position, encourage or convince, make positive use of rules or values, and demonstrate the ability to get others to believe in and trust you because of your competence and honesty
- **Teamwork:** Contribute your ideas to the group in a positive manner, do your share of the work, encourage team members, resolve differences for the benefit of the team, and responsibly challenge existing procedures or policies.

What are your skills?

Link Your Personality and Career Choice

A commonly used system for examining the link between personality style and career choice was developed by John Holland (1997). Holland believes that there are six basic personality types: realistic, investigative, artistic, social, enterprising, and conventional. Following is a description of each, linked with some appropriate careers.

- *Realistic.* People who have athletic or mechanical ability, prefer to work with objects, machines, tools, plants or animals, or to be outdoors. They are less social, and have difficulty in demanding situations. This personality type matches up best with jobs in labor, construction and engineering.
- *Investigative.* People who like to observe, learn, investigate, analyze, evaluate, or solve problems. They are interested in ideas more than people, and are often aloof and intelligent. This personality type matches up with scientific, intellectually oriented professions.
- *Artistic.* People who have artistic, innovative, or intuitional abilities and like to work in unstructured situations using their imagination and creativity. They enjoy working with ideas and materials that allow them to express themselves in innovative ways. They value freedom and ambiguity. Sometimes they have difficulty in social relationships. Not many jobs match up with the artistic type. Consequently, some artistic individuals work in jobs that are second and third choices and then express their artistic interests through hobbies.
- *Social.* People who like to work with other people to enlighten, inform, help, train, or cure them, or are skilled with words. They tend to have a helping orientation and like doing social things more than engaging in intellectual tasks. This personality type matches up with jobs in teaching, social work, and counseling.
- *Enterprising.* People who like to work with people, influencing, persuading, performing, leading, or managing for organizational goals or economic gain. They may try to dominate others and are often good at persuading others. The enterprising type matches up with jobs in sales, management, and politics.
- *Conventional.* People who like to work with data, have clerical or numerical ability, carry out tasks in detail or follow through on others' instructions. The conventional type matches up with jobs in accounting and banking.

Most people are a combination of two or three types, a fact that Holland's system takes into account in matching up a person's type with careers.

Get Experience

As a student, you can participate in part-time or summer work, internships, and cooperative education (co-op) programs relevant to your field of study. This experience can be critical in helping you obtain the job you want when you graduate. Many of today's employers expect job candidates to have this type of experience.

Explore Relevant Part-Time and Summer Jobs

College students benefit more when their jobs are on campus rather than off. This apparently keeps students more in touch with campus life and it takes them less time to commute to their job. Also, on-campus jobs are more likely to be linked with academic pursuits. A good strategy for finding out about on-campus jobs is to go to the financial aid office at your college and ask for a list of available part-time positions. See if any of them will help you develop skills for a future career.

Most departments on a college campus hire student assistants, usually to perform specialized duties such as website design, data input, or clerical work. If you are interested in a major and career in psychology or biology, you might want to go to these departments and ask if any student assistant jobs are available.

With advanced planning, summer jobs can provide good opportunities not only to earn money but also to obtain experiences relevant to your major and your career interests. Obtaining this type of summer job can give you a glimpse of the day-to-day workings of a career you might be interested in and provide a better sense of whether this is the type of life work you want to do. Even if you don't find a part-time or summer position that is relevant to your career interests, most jobs allow you to demonstrate work-related skills and a work ethic that any prospective employer would find attractive.

Do an Internship or a Co-op

Many college students wonder: How do I figure out what I want to do? How do I get a job without experience? How do I get experience without a job? What if I spend four years studying in a particular major and it turns out I don't like it? Internships and co-op experiences can help you answer these questions. These are jobs in the real world that are linked to your academic and career interests.

Internships Most internships are part-time jobs that last for about three to six months, although some last longer. The only time that they might be full time is in the summer and you aren't taking summer classes. Some internships pay a little money but most don't include a salary. Nonetheless, they can significantly help you down the road when you begin looking for full-time employment and a career after college. One study found that students who served in internships during college were 15 percent more likely to find employment after graduation, and 70 percent said that they were better prepared for the workplace because of their internship experience (Knouse, Tanner, & Harris, 1999).

Co-ops Co-ops pay a salary (a typical student makes $7,000 a year) and may last more than a year. Many co-op programs offer academic credit. In four-year colleges, you may not be able to pursue a co-op experience until your junior year, whereas in two-year colleges the co-op experience may be available to both first- and second-year students.

In a national survey of employers, almost 60 percent said their entry-level college hires had co-op or internship experience (Collins, 1996). More than 1,000 colleges in the United States offer cooperative education programs.

Co-ops and internships let you test your career objectives. They can also help you identify your talents and acquire valuable skills that you may need in a future career. Before seeking a particular co-op or internship, ask yourself these questions:

What type of work do I want to do?

In what field?

In what type of organization do I want to work?

What skills do I want to gain from the work experience?

Engage in Service Learning

A wide range of life experiences during college may also help you explore your values related to careers. One example is *service learning*, which involves engaging in activities that promote social responsibility and service to the community (Sherrod & Brabeck, 2002). In service learning, you might tutor, help older adults, volunteer in a hospital, assist in a day care center, or clean up a vacant lot to make a play area.

Why should you participate in service learning during your college years? Researchers have found that when students participate in service learning:

- Their grades improve, they become more motivated, and they set more goals (Johnson & others, 1998).
- Their self-esteem improves (Giles & Eyler, 1998).
- They become less self-centered (Santilli, Falbo, & Harris, 2002).
- They increasingly reflect on society's moral order and social concerns (Metz & McLellan, 2000).

Set Career Goals

Once you have decided on one or more careers that you would like to pursue, it is helpful to think about some long-term and short-term goals. It is important that you be able to articulate these goals to employers and interviewers. The kind of information you should think about incorporating in your career goal setting includes (OCS Basics, 2002):

- major career field target
- preferred type of work, including the ideas or issues you would like to pursue
- income requirements
- geographical requirements (city, rural, mobility, near home, climate, and so on)
- special needs (training, management development, advancement opportunities, career flexibility, entrepreneurial opportunity, and so on)
- industry preferences (manufacturing, government, communications, non-profit, high tech, products, services, and so on)

Explore Career Connections

Career exploration involves investigating the world of work and becoming knowledgeable about different careers. Think about what type of work you are likely to find rewarding and satisfying. This involves exploring different job opportunities while still in college as well as conducting research to gather information from many sources about different fields, industries, and companies.

Explore the *Occupational Outlook Handbook*

As you explore the type of work you are likely to enjoy and in which you can succeed, it is important to be knowledgeable about different fields and companies. Occupations may have many job openings one year but few another year, as economic conditions change. Thus, it is critical to keep up with the occupational outlook in various fields. An excellent source for doing this is the *Occupational Outlook Handbook,* which is revised every two years. Based on the 2004–2005 edition, service industries are expected to provide the greatest number of new jobs, with professional and related occupations projected to increase by the highest rates.

Approximately three fourths of the job growth will come from three groups of professional occupations: computer and mathematical occupations, health practitioners and technical occupations, and education, training, and library occupations.

Projected job growth varies widely by educational requirements. Jobs that require a college degree are expected to grow the fastest. Education is essential to getting a high-paying job. All but one of the 50 highest paying occupations require a college degree.

You can access the *Occupational Outlook Handbook* online at http://www.bls.gov/oco/home.htm. The handbook provides excellent information for a wide range of occupations about what workers do on the job, working conditions, required training and education, and expected job prospects. Libraries are also good sources for finding more about careers. You might want to ask a librarian at your college or university to help you with your career information search.

Connect with Several Careers, Not Just One

When you begin searching for the right career, it's good to have several careers in mind rather than just one. In a recent national survey of first-year college students, only 14 percent believed that they were likely to change their major field of interest (Sax & others, 2003). In reality, far more than this will. Thus, it pays to be knowledgeable about more than just one career field. It also pays to develop a wide variety of general skills, such as communication, that will serve you well in various fields.

Network Networking involves making contact and exchanging information with other people. Check with people you know—your family, friends, people in the community, and alumni—about career information. They might be able to answer your questions themselves or put you in touch with people who can. For example, most college career centers have the names of alumni on file who are willing to talk with students about careers and their work. Networking can lead to meeting someone who can answer your questions about a specific career or company. This is an effective way to learn about the type of training necessary for a particular position, how to enter the field, and what employees like and don't like about their jobs.

Network to meet people who can educate you about careers and introduce you to prospective employers.

Networking is also valuable in a job search and is especially helpful in finding out about nonpublicized job openings. When you network, you can ask for suggestions of people that you might contact for information about job or internship possibilities. The personal contact gained through networking can enhance your chance of getting a job compared to someone who applies as a total stranger.

making connections   Networking

These are some good strategies for networking effectively (OCS Basics, 2002):

Use a wide net and network wherever you go.
People you can network with: everybody. This includes professors, guest speakers, people in line at the coffee shop, your parents, their friends, neighbors, high school teachers, tutors, lab supervisors, alumni of your high school and college, and staff members of community organizations.

Be well prepared.
Be able to clearly spell out as much as you know about what you are looking for in a job.

Always be professional, courteous, considerate, and gracious.
Write a thank you letter when people take the time to meet with you.

Give back.
Know enough about the people you meet when networking to keep their needs in mind. You may be able to pass along ideas, articles, and contacts that will interest them.

See a Career Counselor You might want to talk with a career counselor at your college. This professional is trained to help you discover your strengths and weaknesses, evaluate your values and goals, and help you figure out what type of career is best for you. The counselor will not tell you what to do. You might be asked to take an interest inventory, which the counselor can interpret to help you explore various career options.

Scope Out Internet Resources The dramatic growth of websites has made instantly available countless resources for job possibilities and careers. Most companies, professional societies, academic institutions, and government agencies maintain Internet sites that highlight their latest information and activities.

The range of career information on the Internet tends to overlap with what is available through libraries, career centers, and guidance offices. However, no single network or resource is likely to contain all of the information you're searching for, so explore different sources. As in a library search, look through various lists by field or discipline or by using keywords.

Land a Great Job

Much of what employers look for in top job candidates (such as relevant experience) takes time to acquire. So it's a good idea to start early. As a first-year student, you can begin your career planning process by focusing on obtaining work-related experience, good grades, computer skills, leadership positions, and participation in campus or extracurricular activities.

Research the Job

The more you know about the job, the stronger a candidate you will become. What are the job requirements? What skills and experience are needed? What is the company's philosophy? Check out ads in newspapers and use web resources related to your interests and skills. If you are looking outside of your geographic area, arrange to receive any newspapers that include job listings, or read them on the web. Two websites stand out for their benefits in a job search: *The Riley Guide* (http://www.rileyguide.com) and *JobHuntersBible.com* (http://www.jobhuntersbible.com).

Create a Résumé and Write Letters

Almost all jobs require a *résumé,* a clear and concise description of your interests, skills, experiences, and responsibilities in work, service, extracurricular, and academic settings. Résumés come in a number of different styles and no particular one is considered universally the best. Use white paper, a 10–12 font size, and black type. No errors—misspelled words, grammatical errors, typos—whatsoever should appear in your résumé. Also, your résumé must be an accurate reflection of your job history and accomplishments. Lies on your résumé will catch up with you.

Three types of résumés are most commonly used (OCS Basics, 2002). A *chronological* résumé describes your experiences in reverse chronological order, beginning with your most recent experiences. A *functional* résumé highlights your marketable skills by organizing your accomplishments by skill or career area. This format may be the best choice if you have limited work experience related to the job for which you are applying. Finally, a résumé organized by *achievement* highlights prior work or academic accomplishments. It can be used as an alternative to the first two formats when your accomplishments are centered on a particular skill or experience category.

Most résumés include the following parts (Writers Workshop, 2002):

- *Name:* Centered and boldface font.
- *Address:* Present and permanent, with phone number and/or e-mail address.
- *Job Objective:* This summarizes your reason for submitting a résumé (the position you desire) and your qualifications.
- *Educational Record:* Begin with your most recent education (college you are now attending) and list all schools attended and degrees earned since high school. Indicate your major and areas of specialization. Include your GPA if you have a B average or better, and any honors you have received.

- *Employment History:* List the dates, job title, and organization involved in each job you have held. Begin with the most recent job and conclude with your first. Briefly describe each job, the tasks you performed, the skills you acquired, any special responsibilities or projects, and promotions or achievements.

- *Special Skills:* List any skills you have that are relevant to the job you want but are not mentioned elsewhere on the résumé—for example, expertise with specific software packages or fluency in foreign languages.

- *Professional Affiliations/Activities:* List your membership in any professional organizations and any active role or office you have held. Do not include personal interests or leisure activities.

- *Honors and Awards:* List any honors you have earned or awards you have received since high school.

- *References:* Don't include references on your résumé. State "References available upon request" and take a typed list of two to four references (name, title, organization, relationship, address, and phone number) with you to any job interview.

You will have to write several types of letters during your job search. The most important are the cover letter and the thank-you letter.

A cover letter introduces you to a potential employer. You should never send a résumé to a potential employer without a cover letter. The cover letter briefly describes your qualifications, motivation, and interest in the job. Don't just repeat information in the résumé. Rather, come up with fresh phrases and sentences related to your experiences, skills, and the job you want.

Also get in the habit of writing thank-you letters to the people related to your job search within 24 hours of meeting them. This might be done after an informational meeting with someone you have networked with and should always follow a job interview. It might be tempting to follow up with an e-mail, as it tends to be more efficient. However, a more formal letter sent through "snail mail" is much more impressive and memorable. Don't cut corners here.

Impress Employers in Job Interviews

A key step in getting the job you want is to perform well in an interview. Following are some strategies for success (Yate, 2005):

- *Be prepared.* Interviewers ask for detailed examples of your past experience. They figure you'll do as well on the new job as the old one, so the examples you give can seal your fate.

- *Know your résumé.* Résumés are important. Employers use them to decide whether they want to interview you in the first place and will often ask questions about what they contain. Organize your résumé, write it clearly, and avoid jargon.

- *Don't wing the interview.* Find out as much about your prospective employer as possible. What does the company do? How successful is it? Employers are impressed by applicants who have taken the time to learn about their organization.

Practice interviews will help you keep your cool during the real thing.

- *Anticipate what questions you'll be asked.* Do some practice interviews. Typical interview questions include "What is your greatest strength?" "What interests you the most about this job?" "Why should I hire you?"
- *Ask appropriate job-related questions.* Review the job's requirements with the interviewer.
- *Keep your cool.* Always leave in the same polite way you entered.
- *Decide whether you want the job.* If so, ask for it. Tell the interviewer that you're excited about the job and that you can do it competently. If it isn't offered on the spot, ask when the two of you can talk again.
- *Follow up.* Immediately after the interview, send your follow-up letter. Keep it short—less than one page. Mail it within 24 hours of the interview.

Applying the Six Strategies for Success

How does the material in this chapter make you think about ways you can succeed in college, particularly in terms of exploring and planning your career? Write down your personal insights from reading the chapter that help you make meaningful links to the six strategies for success described on page 111.

Putting It All Together

1. Consider your opinions about different careers. For example:
   - Are some people born to be engineers or nurses? Why or why not?
   - Did your parents shape your career interests?
   - Do your teachers influence your career interests?
   - What kind of an impact can mentors have on a career choice?
   - Are economic factors important to you?
   - What values are most important and why?

2. List a few important ways to evaluate the career(s) you want to pursue.

3. What are some of the most effective ways to acquire work experience while you are still in college?

4. Describe some advantages of networking and using the Internet to explore career opportunities.

5. List three different strategies for creating a strong résumé. Which one do you think will work best for you?

6. In your journal or on paper to turn in, write down your ideal occupation choice. Describe the degree you'll need for your ideal job, such as an A.A., B.A., M.A., or Ph.D. How many years will this take? On a scale of 1 to 10, estimate your chances of obtaining your ideal job. What can you do now to increase your chances of obtaining this career?

Putting It All Together

How has the term or year gone so far? Are you mastering college? Have you put to good use many of the strategies we have described? It's always good to take stock periodically of where you are now, how things have gone, and where you're headed.

Revisit Your Strategies

At the end of the Introduction, you were asked to evaluate where you stand with regard to implementing the six strategies for success in your own life. Now revisit the statements listed below, placing a checkmark next to each one that represents you and your actions now. Leave the others blank. When you are done, go back and award yourself one point for each checkmark. Then add up the points for each of the six sections. Finally, shade the "Strategies for Success" model at the end of this section with your *total* for each of the six strategies. How does this visual model of your strengths and weaknesses compare with that in the Introduction?

Develop Meaningful Values

1. ____ I know what my values are.
2. ____ I feel good about my values.
3. ____ I have reflected on what values I want to guide my life.
4. ____ I have discussed my values with others.
5. ____ My values are helping me succeed in college.
6. ____ My values serve as a foundation for the goals I want to achieve.
7. ____ I've been in situations where my values have been tested and I stayed with them.
8. ____ I have a clear understanding of my purpose in life.
9. ____ I am flexible and realize that my values might change.
10. ____ My values are at the core of my existence.
    TOTAL ____

Set Goals, Plan, and Monitor

1. ____ I am good at setting goals.
2. ____ I have established some long-term goals.
3. ____ I have created subgoals to go along with my long-term goals.
4. ____ The goals I have set are challenging but reachable.
5. ____ My goals are concrete and specific.
6. ____ I periodically monitor my progress toward reaching the goals I have set.
7. ____ I have set completion dates for these goals.
8. ____ I manage time effectively in the pursuit of my goals.
9. ____ I make lists of things I need to do to stay on track in reaching my goals.
10. ____ I anticipate and overcome obstacles on the way to reaching my goals.
        TOTAL ____

Get Motivated and Take Responsibility

1. ____ I am internally motivated.
2. ____ I take responsibility for my actions.
3. ____ I expect to succeed.
4. ____ I am persistent at completing important tasks.
5. ____ I am passionate about succeeding in life.
6. ____ I put a lot of energy into college.
7. ____ I have a strong work ethic.
8. ____ If I get bored, it doesn't last long.
9. ____ I have a strong desire to be a competent person.
10. ____ I am good at staying on task and not being distracted from what I need to do.
        TOTAL ____

Think and Learn

1. ____ I am self-disciplined and have good work habits.
2. ____ I have good study skills.
3. ____ I know the best ways I can learn.
4. ____ I am good at managing my time.
5. ____ I think critically.
6. ____ I think creatively.
7. ____ I have good problem-solving skills.
8. ____ I communicate effectively with good speaking and listening skills.
9. ____ I know what learning resources are available to me and how best to use them.
10. ____ I have good computer skills.
        TOTAL ____

Build Self-Esteem and Confidence

1. ____ I have a lot of confidence in myself.
2. ____ I feel good about myself.
3. ____ I have a positive self-image.
4. ____ I have a lot to be proud of.
5. ____ I am a person of worth.
6. ____ When I don't feel good about myself, I can tell why and attempt to do something about it.
7. ____ If I start to feel bad about myself, it doesn't last long.
8. ____ I have a good support system and get good feedback from others.
9. ____ My achievements help me feel good about myself.
10. ____ I have good coping skills.
    TOTAL ____

Explore Careers

1. ____ I know how much more successful I am likely to be if I complete college.
2. ____ I have several careers that I would like to pursue.
3. ____ I know what my college major will be.
4. ____ My college major matches up well with the careers I am interested in.
5. ____ I have good communication skills.
6. ____ I have good personal skills, including being able to get along with others.
7. ____ I know which college experiences will help me down the road in my pursuit of a career.
8. ____ I have talked with a career counselor about careers that might interest me.
9. ____ I have set some career goals.
10. ____ I am on the right path to reaching those career goals.
    TOTAL ____

Where Are You Now?

You've just done quite a bit of reflecting about some important aspects of life. How do you feel about where you are now? Did you place a checkmark next to most of the areas listed above, or did you leave many of these blank, feeling that you need to improve? If you checked off most of the strategies above, you're likely well on your way to mastering college and developing critical skills that will help you in life after college. If you left many of the spaces blank, this is a good time to reevaluate what your values are and where you can improve.

You have a lot of change ahead of you. Developing meaningful values, setting and monitoring goals, getting motivated and taking responsibility, thinking and learning, building self-esteem and confidence, and exploring careers will continue to be very important themes for you in mastering the remainder of your college years and thereafter. We wish you all the best. We have enjoyed communicating with you this term and hope that as a result of this course and book you feel well on your way to mastering college success.

References

A

Alberti, R., & Emmons, M. (1995). *Your perfect right* (7th ed.). San Luis Obispo, CA: Impact.

Alverno College. (1995). *Writing and speaking criteria.* Milwaukee, WI: Alverno Productions.

American Psychological Association. (2002). *Controlling anger—before it controls you.* Retrieved from http://www.apa.org/pubinfo/anger.html

Anderson, L. W., & Krathwohl, D. R. (Eds.). (2001). *A taxonomy for learning, teaching, and assessment: A revision of Bloom's taxonomy of educational objectives.* New York: Longman.

Appleby, D. (1990). Faculty and student perceptions of irritating behaviors in the college classroom. *Journal of Staff, Program, and Organizational Development, 8,* 41–46.

Appleby, D. (1994). *Liberal arts skills at work* [Career Currents]. Hanover, IN: Hanover College.

Appleby, D. (1997, February). *The seven wonders of the advising world.* Invited address at the Southeastern Teachers of Psychology Conference, Kennesaw State University, Marietta, GA.

Armstrong, W. H., & Lampe, M. W. (1990). *Pocket guide to study tips* (3rd ed.). Hauppage, NY: Barron's Educational Series.

Astin, A. (1993). *What matters in college: Four critical years revisited.* San Francisco: Jossey-Bass.

Axelrod, R. B., & Cooper, C. R. (1996). *The concise guide to writing* (2nd ed.). Boston: Bedford/St. Martin's Press.

B

Bachar, K., & Koss, M. (2001). Rape. In J. Worell (Ed.), *Encyclopedia of women and gender.* San Diego, CA: Academic Press.

Bachman, J. G., O'Malley, P. M., Schulenberg, J. E., Johnston, L. D., Bryant, A. L., & Merline, A. C. (2002). *The decline of substance use in young adulthood.* Mahwah, NJ: Erlbaum.

Bailey, C. (1991). *The new fit or fat* (Rev. ed.). Boston: Houghton Mifflin.

Bandura, A. (2000). Self-efficacy. In A. Kazdin (Ed.), *Encyclopedia of psychology.* Washington, DC and New York: American Psychological Association and Oxford University Press.

Bandura, A. (2001). Social cognitive theory. *Annual Review of Psychology, 53.* Palo Alto, CA: Annual Reviews.

Bashaw, R. E., & Grant, E. S. (1994). Exploring the distinctive nature of work commitments. *Journal of Personal Selling and Sales Management, 14,* 41–56.

Baumrind, D. (1991). Parenting styles and adolescent development. In J. Brooks-Gunn, R. Lerner, & A. C. Petersen (Eds.), *The encyclopedia of adolescence.* New York: Garland.

Baxter Magolda, M. B. (1992). *Knowing and reasoning in college.* San Francisco: Jossey-Bass.

Bednar, R. L., Wells, M. G., & Peterson, S. R. (1995). *Self-esteem* (2nd ed.). Washington, DC: American Psychological Association.

Beck, J. (2002). Beck therapy approach. In M. Hersen, & W. H. Sledge (Eds.), *Encyclopedia of Psychotherapy.* San Diego, CA: Academic Press.

Bennett, M. E., & Miller, W. R. (1998). Alcohol problems. In H. S. Friedman (Ed.), *Encyclopedia of mental health: Vol. 1.* San Diego, CA: Academic Press.

Beyer, G. (1998). *Improving student thinking.* Boston: Allyn & Bacon.

Biasco, F., Goodwin, E. A., & Vitale, K. L. (2001). College students' attitudes toward racial discrimination. *College Student Journal, 35,* 523–529.

Blonna, R. (2005). *Coping with stress in a changing world* (3rd ed.). New York: McGraw-Hill.

Bloom, B. S., Englehart, M. D., Furst, E. J., & Krathwohl, D. R. (1956). *Taxonomy of educational objectives: Cognitive domain.* New York: David McKay.

Bly, R. (1990). *Iron John.* New York: Vintage Books.

Bolles, R. (2002). *What color is your parachute?* Berkeley, CA: Ten Speed Press.

Bolles, R. (2005). *What color is your parachute?* Berkeley, CA: Ten Speed Press.

Bourne, E. J. (1995). *The anxiety and phobia workbook* (2nd ed.). Oakland, CA: New Harbinger Publications.

Boyer Commission. (1998). *Reinventing undergraduate education: A blueprint for America's research universities.* Retrieved June 2002, from http://naples.cc. sunysb.edu/ Pres/boyer.nsf

Bransford, J. D., & Stein, B. S. (1984). *The ideal problem solver.* New York: Freeman.

Brissette, I., Scheier, M. F., & Carver, C. S. (2002). The role of optimism in social network development, coping, and psychological adjustment during a life transition. *Journal of Personality and Social Psychology, 82,* 102–111.

Brislin, R. W. (1993). *Understanding culture's influence on behavior.* Fort Worth, TX: Harcourt Brace.

Brown, F. C., & Buboltz, W. C., Jr. (2002). Applying sleep research to university students: Recommendations for developing a student sleep education program. *Journal of College Student Development, 43,* 411–416.

Brown, F. C., Buboltz, W. C., Jr., & Soper, B. (2001). Prevalence of delayed sleep phase syndrome in university students. *College Student Journal, 35,* 472–476.

Browne, M. N., & Keeley, S. M. (1990). *Asking the right questions: A guide to critical thinking* (3rd ed.). Englewood Cliffs, NJ: Prentice Hall.

Brownell, K. (2000). Dieting. In A. Kazdin (Ed.), *Encyclopedia of psychology.* Washington, DC and New York: American Psychological Association and Oxford University Press.

C

Cacioppo, J. T. (2002). Emotion and health. In R. J. Davidson, K. R. Sherer, & H. H. Goldsmith (Eds.), *Handbook of affective sciences.* New York: Oxford University Press.

Canfield, J., & Hansen, N. V. (1995). *The Aladdin factor.* New York: Berkeley.

Carskadon, M. A. (1990). Patterns of sleep and sleepiness in adolescence. *Pediatrics, 17,* 5–12.

CNET Tech. (2002). *When games stop being fun.* Retrieved from http://news.com.com/2100-1040-881673.html

Collins, M. (1996, Winter). The job outlook for '96 grads. *Journal of Career Planning,* 51–54.

Combs, P. (2002). *Major in success* (3rd ed.). Berkeley, CA: Ten Speed Press.

Consumer Credit Counseling Service of Greater Dallas, Inc. (2000). *Credit: Information for today's consumer.* (Credit Seminar Workbook). Dallas, TX: New Vision Technologies, Inc.

Costa, P. T., & McCrae, R. R. (1995). Solid grounds in the wetlands of personality: A replay to Block. *Psychological Bulletin, 117,* 216–220.

Courtenay, W. H., McCreary, D. R., & Merighi, J. R. (2002). Gender and ethnic differences in health beliefs and behaviors. *Journal of Health Psychology, 7,* 219–231.

Covey, S. R. (1989). *The seven habits of highly effective people.* New York: Simon & Schuster.

Covey, S. R., Merrill, A. R., & Merrill, R. R. (1994). *First things first.* New York: Simon & Schuster.

Crooks, R., & Bauer, K. (2002). *Our sexuality* (8th ed.). Pacific Grove, CA: Brooks/Cole.

Crooks, R., & Bauer, K. (2004). *Our sexuality* (9th ed.). Belmont, CA: Wadsworth.

Csikszentmihalyi, M. (1995). *Creativity.* New York: HarperCollins.

Csikszentmihalyi, M. (1997). *Finding flow.* New York: Basic Books.

Cutrona, C. E. (1982). Transition to college: Loneliness and the process of social adjustment. In L. A. Peplau, & D. Perlman (Eds.), *Loneliness: A sourcebook of current theory, research, and therapy.* New York: Wiley.

D

Davis, M., Eshelman, E. R., & McKay, M. (2000). *The relaxation and stress reduction workbook* (5th ed.). Oakland, CA: New Harbinger Publications.

Davis, S. F., Grover, C. A., Becker, A. H., & McGregor, L. N. (1992). Academic dishonesty: Prevalence, determinants, techniques, and punishments. *Teaching of Psychology, 19,* 16–20.

DeFleur, M. L., Kearning, P., Plax, T., & DeFleur, M. H. (2005). *Fundamentals of human communication* (3rd ed.). New York: McGraw-Hill.

DeLongis, A., & Newth, S. (1998). Coping with stress. In H. S. Friedman (Ed.), *Encyclopedia of mental health: Vol. 1.* San Diego, CA: Academic Press.

Dement, W. C., & Vaughn, C. (2000). *The promise of sleep.* New York: Dell.

Diener, E., & Seligman, M. E. P. (2002). Very happy people. *Psychological Science, 13,* 81–84.

DeVito, J. (2004). *Interpersonal communication workbook* (10th ed.). Upper Saddle River, NJ: Prentice Hall.

E

Economos, C. (2001). Unpublished manuscript: *Tufts longitudinal health study.* Medford, MA: Center on Nutrition Communication.

Edelman, M. W. (1992). *The measure of our success.* Boston: Beacon Press.

Eggers, D. (2000). Commentary in Combs, P. *Major in success* (3rd ed.). Berkeley, CA: Ten Speed Press.

Eggers, D. (2000). *A heartbreaking work of staggering genius.* New York: Vintage Books.

Eggert, L. L., Thomspon, F. A., Randell, B. P., & Pike, K. C. (2002). Preliminary effects of brief school-based prevention approaches of reducing youth suicide—risk behaviors, depression, and drug involvement. *Journal of Child and Adolescent Psychiatric Nursing, 15,* 48–64.

Elliott, M. (1999). *Time, work, and meaning.* Unpublished doctoral dissertation, Pacifica Graduate Institute.

Ellis, A. (1996). A rational-emotive behavior therapist's perspective on Ruth. In G. Corey (Ed.), *Case approach to counseling and psychotherapy.* Pacific Grove, CA: Brooks/Cole.

Ellis, A. (2002). Rational emotive behavior therapy. In M. Herson, & W. H. Sledge (Eds.), *Encyclopedia of psychotherapy.* San Diego, CA: Academic Press.

Epstein, R. L. (2000). *The pocket guide to critical thinking.* Belmont, CA: Wadsworth.

F

Farr, J. M. (1999). *America's top jobs for college graduates.* Indianapolis, IN: JIST Works.

Frank, S. (1996). *The everything study book.* Holbrook, MA: Adams Media.

Fulghum, R. (1997). Pay attention. In R. Carlson, & B. Shield (Eds.), *Handbook for the soul.* Boston: Little, Brown.

Folkman, S., & Moskowitz, J. T. (2004). Coping: Pitfalls and promises. *Annual Review of Psychology, Vol. 55.* Palo Alto, CA: Annual Reviews.

G

Garner, P. W., & Estep, K. M. (2001). Empathy and emotional expressivity. In J. Worell (Ed.), *Encyclopedia of women and gender.* San Diego, CA: Academic Press.

Gardner, H. (1989). *Frames of mind.* New York: Basic Books.

Gardner, H. (1999). *The disciplined mind.* New York: Simon & Schuster.

Gewertz, K. (2000). *Harvard University Gazette.* Retrieved from http://www.news.harvard.edu/gazette/2000/06.08/ellison.html

Giles, D. E., Jr., & Eyler, J. (1998). A service learning research agenda for the next five years. *New Directions for Teaching and Learning, 73,* 65–72.

Goldberg, H. (1980). *The new male.* New York: Signet.

Goleman, D., Kaufmann, P., & Ray, M. (1992). *The creative spirit.* New York: Plume.

Gordon, T. (1970). *Parent effectiveness training.* New York: McGraw-Hill.

Gottman, J., & Silver, N. (1999). *The seven principles for making marriages work.* New York: Crown.

Grandin, T. (1995). *Thinking in pictures.* New York: Doubleday.

Griffith-Joyner, F., & Hanc, J. (1999). *Running for dummies.* Foster City, CA: IDG Books.

H

Haag, S., & Perry, J. T. (2003). *Internet Explorer 6.0.* New York: McGraw-Hill.

Haines, M. E., Norris, M. P., & Kashy, D. A. (1996). The effects of depressed mood on academic performance in college students. *Journal of College Student Development, 37,* 519–526.

Halberg, E., Halberg, K., & Sauer, L. (2000). *Success factors index.* Auburn, CA: Ombudsman Press.

Halonen, J. S., & Brown-Anderson, F. (2002). Teaching thinking. In W. J. McKeachie, *Teaching Tips* (11th ed.). Boston: Houghton Mifflin.

Halonen, J. S., & Gray, C. (2001). *The critical thinking companion for introductory psychology.* New York: Worth Publishers.

Halpern, D. F. (1997). *Critical thinking across the curriculum.* Mahwah, NJ: Erlbaum.

Hamburg, D. A. (1997). Meeting the essential requirements for healthy adolescent development in a transforming world. In R. Takanishi, & D. Hamburg (Eds.), *Preparing adolescents for the twenty-first century.* New York: Cambridge University Press.

Hansen, R. S., & Hansen, K. (1997). *Write your way to a higher GPA.* Berkeley, CA: Ten Speed Press.

Harbin, C. E. (1995). *Your transfer planner.* Belmont, CA: Wadsworth.

Harris, R. A. (2001). *The plagiarism handbook: Strategies for preventing, detecting, and dealing with plagiarism.* Los Angeles: Pyrczak Publishing.

Harter, S. (2006). The self. In W. Damon, & R. Lerner (Eds.), *Handbook of child psychology* (6th ed.). New York: Wiley.

Heinrich, R., Molenda, M., Russell, J. D., & Smaldino, S. E. (2002). *Instructional media and technologies for learning* (7th ed.). Upper Saddle River, NJ: Prentice Hall.

Hersen, M., & Sledge, W. H. (Eds.) (2002). *Encyclopedia of psychotherapy.* San Diego, CA: Academic Press.

Hicks, R. A., & Pellegrini, R. J. (1991). The changing sleep habits of college students. *Perceptual and Motor Skills, 72,* 1106.

Hillman, R. (1999). *Delivering dynamic presentations: Using your voice and body for impact.* Needham Heights, NJ: Allyn & Bacon.

Hofstetter, F. T. (2003). *Internet literacy.* New York: McGraw-Hill.

Holland, J. (1997). *Making vocational choices.* Lutz, FL: Psychological Assessment Resources.

Howatt, W. A. (1999). Journaling to self-evaluation: A tool for adult learners. *International Journal of Reality Therapy, 18,* 32–34.

Hurtado, S., Dey, E. L., & Trevino, J. G. (1994). *Exclusion or self-segregation? Interaction across racial/ethnic groups on college campuses.* Paper presented at the meeting of the American Educational Research Association, New York.

Hyde, J. S., & DeLamater, J. D. (2005). *Understanding human sexuality* (8th ed.). New York: McGraw-Hill.

I

Insel, P. M., & Roth, W. T. (2002). *Core concepts of health* (9th ed.). New York: McGraw-Hill.

Ishikawa, K. (1986). *What is total quality control? The Japanese way.* Englewood Cliffs, NJ: Prentice Hall.

J

Jandt, F. E. (2004). *An introduction to intercultural communication.* Thousand Oaks, CA: Sage.

Jendrick, M. P. (1992). Students' reactions to academic dishonesty. *Journal of College Student Development, 33,* 260–273.

Johnson, M. K., Beebe, T., Mortimer, J. T., & Snyder, M. (1998). Volunteerism in adolescence: A process perspective. *Journal of Research in Adolescence, 8,* 309–332.

Johnston, L. D., O'Malley, P. M., & Bachman, J. G. (1996). *National survey results on drug use from the Monitoring the Future study, 1975–1994: Vol. 2.* Rockville, MD: National Institute on Drug Abuse.

Johnston, L., O'Malley, G., & Bachman, J. (2004). *Monitoring the Future.* Ann Arbor, MI: Institute of Social Research.

Jonassen, D. H., & Grabowski, B. L. (1993). *Handbook of individual differences, learning, and instruction.* Mahwah, NJ: Erlbaum.

K

Kagan, J. (1965). Reflection-impulsivity and reading development in primary grade children. *Child Development, 36,* 609–628.

Kaplan, R. M., & Saccuzzo, D. P. (1993). *Psychological testing: Principles, applications, and issues* (3rd ed.). Pacific Grove, CA: Brooks/Cole.

Kappes, S. (2001). *The truth about Janeane Garofalo.* Retrieved from http://people.aol.com/people/features/celebrityspotlight/0,10950,169561,00.html

Keith-Spiegel, P. (1992, October). *Ethics in shades of pale gray.* Paper presented at the Mid-America Conference for Teachers of Psychology, Evansville, IN.

Keller, P. A., & Heyman, S. R. (1987). *Innovations in clinical practice.* Sarasota, FL: Professional Resource Exchange.

Kelly, J. (2000). Sexually transmitted diseases. In A. Kazdin (Ed.), *Encyclopedia of psychology.* Washington, DC and New York: American Psychological Association and Oxford University Press.

Kierwa, K. A. (1987). Note-taking and review: The research and its implications. *Instructional Science, 19,* 394–397.

King, A. (2000). Exercise and physical activity. In A. Kazdin (Ed.), *Encyclopedia of psychology.* Washington, DC and New York: American Psychological Association and Oxford University Press.

King, T., & Bannon, E. (2002, April). *At what cost? The price that working students pay for a college education.* Washington, DC: U.S. Department of Education, State Public Interest Research Groups' Higher Education Project.

Knouse, S., Tanner, J., & Harris, E. (1999). The relation of college internships, college performance, and subsequent job opportunity. *Journal of Employment Counseling, 36,* 35–43.

Kolb, D. A. (1984). *Experiential learning: Experience as the source of learning and development.* Englewood Cliffs, NJ: Prentice Hall.

Koss, M., & Boeschen, L. (1998). Rape. In H. S. Friedman (Ed.), *Encyclopedia of mental health: Vol. 3.* San Diego, CA: Academic Press.

Kurose, J. F., & Ross, K. W. (2001). *Computer networking.* Boston: Addison-Wesley.

L

Lack, L. C. (1986). Delayed sleep and sleep loss in university students. *Journal of American College Health, 35,* 105–110.

Lakein, A. (1973). *How to get control of your time and your life.* New York: Signet.

Lane, A. M., Crone-Grant, D., & Lane, H. (2002). Mood changes following exercise. *Perceptual and Motor Skills, 94,* 732–734.

Langer, E. (1997). *The power of mindful learning.* Reading, MA: Addison-Wesley.

Lazarus, R. S. (1993). Coping theory and research: Past, present, and future. *Psychosomatic Medicine, 55,* 234–247.

Lazarus, R. S. (1998). *Fifty years of the research and theory of R. S. Lazarus.* Mahwah, NJ: Erlbaum.

Lerner, H. G. (1989). *The dance of intimacy.* New York: HarperCollins.

Levinger, E. E. (1949). *Albert Einstein.* New York: Julian Messner.

Lin, J. G., & Yi, J. K. (1997). Asian international students' adjustments. *College Student Journal, 31,* 473–479.

Loftus, E. F. (1980). *Memory.* Reading, MA: Addison-Wesley.

Loftus, E. F. (1993). The reality of repressed memories. *American Psychologist, 48,* 518–537.

Lorayne, H., & Lucas, J. (1996). *The memory book.* New York: Ballantine.

M

Maas, J. (1998). *Power sleep: The program that prepares your mind for peak performance.* New York: Villard.

MacKenzie, A. (1997). *The time trap* (3rd ed.). New York: American Management Association.

Marcus, A., Mullins, L. C., Brackett, K. P., Tang, Z., Allen, A. M., & Pruett, D. W. (2003). Perceptions of racism on campus. *College Student Journal, 37,* 611–617.

Maris, R. W. (1998). Suicide. In H. S. Friedman (Ed.), *Encyclopedia of mental health: Vol. 3.* San Diego, CA: Academic Press.

Matlin, M. (1998). *Cognitive psychology* (3rd ed.). New York: Harcourt Brace.

Mayo Clinic (2004). *Special Diets.* Rochester, MN: Author.

McCabe, D. L., & Trevino, L. K. (1993). Academic dishonesty: Honor codes and other contextual influences. *Journal of Higher Education, 64,* 522–538.

McDonald, R. L. (1994). *How to pinch a penny till it screams.* Garden City, NY: Avery.

McKeachie, W. J. (2002). *Teaching Tips* (11th ed.). Boston: Houghton Mifflin.

McKowen, C. (1996). *Get your A out of college: Mastering the hidden rules of the game.* Los Altos, CA: Crisp Publications.

McNally, D. (1990). *Even eagles need a push.* New York: Dell.

McNett, J., Harvey, C., Athanassiou, N., & Allard, J. (2000, July 17). *Bloom's taxonomy as a teaching tool: An experiment.* Paper presented at Improving University Teaching Conference, Frankfurt, Germany.

Mendoza, J. C. (1999). *Resiliency factors in high school students at risk for academic failure.* Unpublished doctoral dissertation, California School of Professional Psychology.

Metz, E., & McLellan, J. A. (2000, April). *Challenging community service predicts civic engagement and social concerns.* Paper presented at the meeting of the Society for Research on Adolescence, Chicago, IL.

Michael, R. T., Gagnon, J. H., Laumann, E. O., & Kolata, G. (1994). *Sex in America.* Boston: Little, Brown.

Miller, G. A. (1956). The magical number seven, plus or minus two: Some limits on our capacity for information-processing. *Psychological Review, 48,* 337–442.

Miller, J. B. (1986). *Toward a new psychology of women* (2nd ed.). Boston: Beacon Press.

Mrosko, T. (2002). *Keys to successful networking.* Retrieved from http://www.iwritesite.com/keys.html

Murphy, M. C. (1996). Stressors on the college campus: A comparison of 1985 and 1993. *Journal of College Student Development, 37,* 20–28.

Mussell, M. P., & Mitchell, J. E. (1998). Anorexia nervosa and bulimia nervosa. In H. S. Friedman (Ed.), *Encyclopedia of mental health: Vol. 1.* San Diego, CA: Academic Press.

Myers, I. E. (1962). *Manual: Myers-Briggs Type Indicator.* Princeton, NJ: Educational Testing Service.

N

Newman, E. (1976). *A civil tongue.* Indianapolis: Bobbs-Merrill.

Nichols, R. B. (1961, March). Do we know how to listen? Practical helps in a modern age. *Speech Teacher, 10,* 22.

Niven, D. (2001). *The 100 simple secrets of successful people.* San Francisco: Harper.

Nolen-Hoeksema, S. (2001). *Abnormal psychology* (2nd ed.). New York: McGraw-Hill.

Nolen-Hoeksema, S. (2004). *Abnormal psychology* (3rd ed.). New York: McGraw-Hill.

O

Occupational Outlook Handbook. (2000–2001). Washington, DC: U.S. Department of Labor.

Occupational Outlook Handbook. (2004). Washington, DC: U.S. Department of Labor.

Occupational Outlook Handbook. (2004–2005). Washington, DC: U.S. Department of Labor.

Occupational Outlook Handbook. (2006–2007). Washington, DC: U.S. Department of Labor.

OCS Basics. (2002). *Job search basics.* Cambridge, MA: Office of Career Services. Retrieved from http://www.ocs.fas.harvard.edu/basics

P

Paludi, M. A. (1998). *The psychology of women.* Upper Saddle River, NJ: Prentice Hall.

Pear, J., & Martin, G. L. (2003). *Behavior modification* (7th ed.). Upper Saddle River, NJ: Prentice Hall.

Peck, M. S. (1978). *The road less traveled.* New York: Touchstone.

Peck, M. S. (1997). *The road less traveled & beyond: Spiritual growth in an age of anxiety.* New York: Simon & Schuster.

Pennebaker, J. W. (1997). *Opening up.* (Rev. ed.). New York: Avon.

Pennebaker, J. W. (2001). Dealing with a traumatic experience immediately after it occurs. *Advances in Mind-Body Medicine, 17,* 160–162.

Pennebaker, J. W. (2002). *Writing and health: Some practical advice.* Retrieved from http://homepage.psy.utexas. edu/homepage/faculty/pennebaker/Pennebaker.html

Perkins, D. N. (1984, September). Creativity by design. *Educational Leadership,* pp. 18–25.

Perlman, D., & Peplau, L. A. (1998). Loneliness. In H. S. Friedman (Ed.), *Encyclopedia of psychology: Vol. 2.* San Diego, CA: Academic Press.

Peterson, C., & Stunkard, A. J. (1986). *Personal control and health promotion.* Unpublished manuscript, Department of Psychology, University of Michigan, Ann Arbor.

Polivy, J., Herman, P., Mills, J., & Brock, H. (2003). Eating disorders in adolescence. In G. Adams, & M. Berzonsky (Eds.), *Blackwell handbook of adolescence.* Malden, MA: Blackwell.

Pomerleau, O. (2000). Smoking. In A. Kazdin (Ed.), *Encyclopedia of psychology.* Washington, DC and New York: American Psychological Association and Oxford University Press.

Poole, B. J. (1998). *Education for an information age* (2nd ed.). Burr Ridge, IL: McGraw-Hill.

Post, G. (2002). *Database management systems.* New York: McGraw-Hill.

R

Raimes, A. (2002). *A brief handbook* (3rd ed.). Boston: Houghton Mifflin.

Robeson, R. (1998). *College students on the rebound.* Unpublished doctoral dissertation. University of Indiana.

Rodin, J., & Langer, E. J. (1977). Long-term effects of a control-relevant intervention with the institutionalized aged. *Journal of Personality and Social Psychology, 35,* 397–402.

Roth, D., Eng, W., & Heimberg, R. G. (2002). Cognitive behavior therapy. In M. Hersen, & W. H. Sledge (Eds.), *Encyclopedia of psychotherapy.* San Diego, CA: Academic Press.

Ruggerio, V. R. (1996). *Becoming a critical thinker* (2nd ed.). Boston: Houghton Mifflin.

S

Santilli, J. S., Falbo, M. C., & Harris, J. T. (2002, April). *The role of volunteer services, self perceptions, and relationships with others on prosocial development.* Paper presented at the meeting of the Society for Research on Adolescence, New Orleans, LA.

Sax, L. J., Astin, A. W., Korn, W. S., & Mahoney, K. M. (1995). *The American college freshman: National norms for fall, 1995.* Los Angeles: Higher Education Research Institute, UCLA.

Sax, L. J., Astin, A. W., Korn, W. S., & Mahoney, K. M. (1999). *The American freshman: National norms for fall 1999.* Los Angeles: Higher Education Research Institute, UCLA.

Sax, L. J., Astin, A. W., Korn, W. S., & Mahoney, K. M. (2000). *The American freshman: National norms for fall 2000.* Los Angeles: Higher Education Research Institute, UCLA.

Sax, L. J., Lindholm, J. A., Astin, A. W., Korn, W. S., & Mahoney, K. M. (2001). *The American freshman: National norms for fall 2001.* Los Angeles: Higher Education Research Institute, UCLA.

Sax, L. J., Astin, A. W., Lindholm, J. A., Korn, W. S., Saenz, V. B., & Mahoney, K. M. (2003). *The American freshman: National norms for fall 2003.* Los Angeles: Higher Education Research Institute, UCLA.

Sax, L. J., Astin, A. W., Lindholm, J. A., Korn, W. S., Saenz, V. B., & Mahoney, K. M. (2004). *The American freshman: National norms for fall 2004.* Los Angeles: Higher Education Research Institute, UCLA.

Scott, R. L., & Cordova, J. V. (2002). The influence of adult attachment styles on the association between marital adjustment and depressive symptoms. *Journal of Family Psychology, 16,* 199–208.

Sears, D. O., Peplau, L. A., & Taylor, S. E. (2003). *Social psychology* (11th ed.). Upper Saddle River, NJ: Prentice Hall.

Sedlacek, W. (1999). Black students on White campuses. *Journal of College Student Development, 40,* 538–550.

Seligman, M. E. P. (1991). *Learned optimism.* New York: Pocket Books.

Shaver, P. R., Belsky, J., & Brennan, K. A. (2000). Comparing measures of adult attachment: An examination of interview and self-report methods. *Personal Relationships, 7,* 25–43.

Sher, K. J., Wood, P. K., & Gotham, H. J. (1996). The course of psychological distress in college: A prospective high-risk study. *Journal of College Student Development, 37,* 42–51.

Sherrod, L., & Brabeck, K. (2002, April). *Community service and youths' political views.* Paper presented at the meeting of the Society for Research on Adolescence, New Orleans, LA.

Skinner, K. (1997). *The MSE Oracle System.* Dallas, TX: Southern Methodist University.

Smolak, L., & Striegel-Moore, R. (2002). Body image concerns. In J. Worell (Ed.), *Encyclopedia of women and gender.* San Diego, CA: Academic Press.

Stark, R. (1994). *Sociology* (5th ed.). Belmont, CA: Wadsworth.

Stern, L., Iqbal, N., Seshadri, P., Chicano, K. L., Daily, D. A., McGrory, J., Williams, M., Gracely, E. J., & Samantha, F. F. (2004). The effects of low-carbohydrate versus conventional weight loss diets in severely obese adults: One-year follow-up of a randomized trial. *Annals of Internal Medicine, 140,* 778–785.

Sternberg, R. J. (1988). *The triangle of love.* New York: Basic Books.

Sternberg, R. J., & Lubart, T. I. (1995). *Defying the crowd: Cultivating creativity in a culture of conformity.* New York: Free Press.

Stipek, D. (2002). *Motivation to learn* (4th ed.). Boston: Allyn & Bacon.

Strong, R. W., Silver, H. F., Perini, M. J., & Tuculescu, G. M. (2002). *Reading for academic success.* Thousand Oaks, CA: Corwin Press.

Stukas, A. A., Clary, E. G., & Snyder, M. (1999). Service learning: Who benefits and why. *Social Policy Report: Vol. 13, no. 4.* Chicago: Society for Research in Child Development.

Swartz, R. (2001). Thinking about decisions. In A. L. Costa (Ed.). *Developing minds: A resource book for teaching thinking.* Alexandria, VA: Association for Supervision and Curriculum Development.

T

Tan, Amy. (1996, June 28). [Interview]. Retrieved from www.achievement.org/autodoc/page/tanoint-1

Tannen, D. (1986). *That's not what I meant!* New York: Ballantine.

Tannen, D. (1990). *You just don't understand!* New York: Ballantine.

Tavris, C. (1989). *Anger: The misunderstood emotion* (2nd ed.). New York: Touchstone.

Tavris, C. (1992). *The mismeasure of woman.* New York: Touchstone.

Taylor, S. E. (2003). *Health psychology* (5th ed.). New York: McGraw-Hill.

Tiene, D., & Ingram, A. (2001). *Exploring current issues in educational technology.* New York: McGraw-Hill.

Treagust, D. F., Duit, R., & Fraser, B. J. (1996). *Improving teaching and learning in science and mathematics.* New York: Teachers College Press.

Tyler, S. (2001). *Been there, should've done that: More tips for making the most of college* (2nd ed.). Michigan: Front Porch Press.

U

University of Illinois Counseling Center. (1984). *Overcoming procrastination.* Urbana-Champaign, IL: Department of Student Affairs.

V

van Praag, H., Kempermann, G., & Gage, F. H. (1999). Running increases cell proliferation and neurogenesis in the adult mouse dentate gyrus. *Nature Neuroscience, 3,* 266–270.

Vickery, D. M., & Fries, J. F. (2000). *Take care of yourself* (7th ed.). Reading, MA: Addison-Wesley.

Voelker, R. (2004). Stress, sleep loss, and substance abuse create potent recipe for college depression. *Journal of the American Medical Association, 291,* 2177–2179.

Von Oech, Roger. (1990). *A whack on the side of the head: How you can be more creative.* New York: Warner.

W

Walters, A. (1994). Using visual media to reduce homophobia: A classroom demonstration. *Journal of Sex Education and Therapy, 20,* 92–100.

Wechsler, H., Davenport, A., Sowdall, G., Moetykens, B., & Castillo, S. (1994). Health and behavioral consequences of binge drinking in college. *Journal of the American Medical Association, 272,* 1672–1677.

Wechsler, H., Lee, J. E., Kuo, M., & Lee, H. (2000). College binge drinking in the 1990s—a continuing health problem: Results from the Harvard University School of Health 1999 College Alcohol Study. *Journal of American College Health, 48,* 1999–2010.

Wechsler, H., Lee, J. E., Kuo, M., Seibring, M., Nelson, T. F., & Lee, H. (2002). Trends in college binge drinking during a period of increased prevention efforts: Findings from Harvard School of Public Health College Alcohol Study surveys: 1993–2001. *Journal of American College Health, 50,* 203–217.

Weinstein, N. D. (1984). Reducing unrealistic optimism about illness susceptibility. *Health Psychology, 3,* 431–457.

Weston Exploration. (2002). *The model for exploration.* Urbana-Champaign, IL: Weston Exploration, University of Illinois. Retrieved from http://www.housing.uiuc.edu/academics/estonex/index.htm

Whimbey, A., & Lochhead, J. (1991). *Problem solving and comprehension.* Mahwah, NJ: Erlbaum.

Whitley, B. E., Jr., & Keith-Spiegel, P. (2002). *Academic dishonesty: An educator's guide.* Mahwah, NJ: Erlbaum.

Wigfield, A., & Eccles, J. S. (Eds.). (2002). *Development of achievement motivation.* San Diego, CA: Academic Press.

Wigfield, A., Eccles, J. S., Schiefele, U., Roeser, R., & Davis-Kean, P. (2006). Development of achievement motivation. In W. Damon, & R. Lenner (Eds.), *Handbook of child psychology* (6th ed.). New York: Wiley.

Winston, S. (1995). *Stephanie Winston's best organizing tips.* New York: Simon & Schuster.

Writers Workshop. (2002). *Writing resumes.* Urbana-Champaign, IL: Center for Writing Studies, University of Illinois. Retrieved from http://www.english.uiuc.edu/

Y

Yager, J. (1999). *Creative time management for the new millennium* (2nd ed.). Stamford, CT: Hannacroix Books.

Yate, M. (2002). *Knock 'em dead.* Boston: Adams Media.

Yate, M. (2005). *Knock 'em dead.* Boston: Adams Media.

Yates, M. (1995, March). *Community service and political-moral discussions among black urban adolescents.* Paper presented at the meeting of the Society for Research in Child Development, Indianapolis, IN.

Young, M. L. (2002). *Internet: The complete reference* (2nd ed.). New York: McGraw-Hill.

Z

Zeidner, M. (1995). Adaptive coping with test situations: A review of the literature. *Educational Psychologist, 30,* 123–133.

Zeurcher-White, E. (1997). *Treating panic disorder and agoraphobia: A step-by-step clinical guide.* Oakland, CA: New Harbinger Publications.PHOTO CREDITS   Connections

Photo Credits

xiii: © Paul Thomas/Getty Images. **xiv:** © Doug Menuez/Getty Images. **xvii:** © Kaz Mori/Getty Images. **xix:** ©Tom Stewart/Corbis. **xxii:** © David Young-Wolff/PhotoEdit. **1:** © Kevin Horan/Getty Images. **3:** © Janine Wiedel Photolibrary/Alamy. **4:** © Purestock/Superstock. **6:** © Royalty Free/Corbis. **9:** © Chuck Savage/Corbis. **11:** © Stephan Simpson/Getty Images. **12:** © Paul Wright/Masterfile. **19:** © Colin Young-Wolff/PhotoEdit. **21:** © Matthias Tunger/Digital-Vision/Getty Images. **23:** © Royalty-Free/Masterfile. **26:** © Martin Meyer/Zefa/Corbis. **31:** © Yellow Dog Productions/Getty Images. **32:** © Doug Menuez/Getty Images. **35:** © Tom Stewart/Corbis. **37:** © Bill Varle/Corbis. **38:** © AP Photo/Joe DeMaria. **41:** © Phil Boorman/Getty Images. **44:** © Jon Feingersh/zefa/Corbis. **46:** © Michael Newman/PhotoEdit. **51:** © Stock4B/Getty Images. **52:** © David Young Wolff/PhotoEdit. **57:** © Robbie Jack/Corbis. **60:** © Royalty Free/Corbis. **61:** © Phil Schofield/Getty Images.

62: © Mary Steinbacher/PhotoEdit. **67:** © David Young-Wolff/PhotoEdit. **68:** © Jacobs Stock Photography/Getty Images. **69:** © Digital Vision/Getty Images. **71:** © Nick White/DigitalVision/Getty Images. **75:** © Image100/Superstock. **77:** © Jiang Jin/Superstock. **79:** © Digital Vision/Getty images. **81:** © White Packert/Getty Images. **82:** © Comstock/Getty Images. **85:** © BananaStock. **87:** © Naile Goelbasi/Getty Images. **89:** © Timothy Allen/Axiom/Aurora. **91:** © Kevin Cooley/Getty Images. **93:** © Richard Schultz/Getty Images. **94:** © Image100/Superstock. **97:** © Emmanuel Faure/Getty Images. **99:** © Marty Heitner/The Image Works. **101:** © Steve Casimiro/Getty Images. **102:** © BananaStock/PictureQuest. **107:** © Mark Peterson/Corbis. **111:** © Michael Newman/PhotoEdit. **111:** © Stockbyte/Getty Images. **113:** © BananaStock/PictureQuest. **114:** © Artiga Photo/Corbis. **117:** © Orbit/Masterfile. **119:** © Comstock Images/Alamy

Index